Disguised as a Poem

Disguised as a Poem

My Years Teaching
Poetry at San Quentin

Judith Tannenbaum

Northeastern University Press
Boston

Northeastern University Press

Library of Congress Cataloging-in-Publication Data
Tannenbaum, Judith.
    Disguised as a poem : my years teaching poetry at San Quentin /
Judith Tannenbaum.
        p.   cm.
    Includes bibliographical references.
    ISBN 1-55553-453-8 (cloth : alk. paper) — ISBN 1-55553-452-X
(pbk. : alk. paper)
    1. Poetry—Study and teaching.   2. Prisoners—Education—California.
I. Title.
    PN1101 .T35 2000
    365'.66—dc21
    [B]   00-041889

Designed by Janis Owens

Composed in Janson by The Composing Room of Michigan, Inc., Grand
Rapids, Michigan. Printed and bound by Edwards Brothers, Inc., Lilling-
ton, North Carolina. The paper is EB Natural, an acid-free stock.

MANUFACTURED IN THE UNITED STATES OF AMERICA
04   03   02   01   00   5   4   3   2   1

For my San Quentin students

contents

Preface / ix
Acknowledgments / xv

one   The First Three Months / 3

two   Cleansing the Doors of Perception / 26

three   "Endless Echoes of Steel Kissing Steel" / 47

four   "You Gotta Walk That Lonesome Valley . . ." / 65

five   "Like a Poet" / 81

six   "In the Very Essence of Poetry There Is
Something Indecent" / 100

seven   Long-Term, In-Depth / 124

eight   "To All Mankind They Were Addressed":
Godot at San Quentin / 146

nine   "Which Side Are You On?" / 162

ten   "Love Begins Right Here in This Place" / 179

Notes / 201

preface

I walked into San Quentin for the first time in May 1985 to recite poems to a group of ten men. I walked out with an offer to teach. For four years—the first on a once-a-week basis, the following three for twenty hours each week—I was poet-in-residence at this maximum security prison.

From Black Bart to George Jackson, a series of folk-hero-bad-guys (and a couple of gals) has shaped the myth of San Quentin. My students weren't myths, though; they weren't heroes or beasts. They were human. During my years at the prison, I watched these men live their lives behind locked gates and cell bars; what I witnessed, as well as what I myself experienced, taught me as much about what it is to be a human being as I taught my students about poetry.

As befitting a myth, San Quentin sits solidly on Point Quentin—a mile-and-one-half-long hook of land that juts into the bay that is called San Francisco to the south and San Pablo to the north. Saint Quentin was a third-century Roman who was beheaded by the Gauls, who first ran iron spits through his body from head to foot. A white dove is said to have risen from his open throat and ascended toward heaven.

The point and the pen, though, were not named for Saint Quentin but after an Indian warrior who fought with the great Chief Marin, the leader of the Coastal Miwoks in their last stand against Mexican troops. In 1824, subchief Quentin was taken prisoner on the hook of land that now bears his name.

Many states and countries have successful prison art programs. Prisons in some states contract with an outside agency to hire art teachers and buy materials. Others provide art classes through their education departments. Elsewhere, teachers from local colleges give arts instruction inside prisons and jails. Often, professional artists volunteer their time.

In California, offering fine arts instruction inside every state prison is the mission of a program called Arts-in-Corrections. A professional artist fills a civil service position at each state prison; his or her job is to put together an arts program for that institution. During most of my years at San Quentin, this artist/facilitator position was filled by Jim Carlson.

Each artist/facilitator contracts with other artists to teach their art forms to prisoners. These artists are funded in a number of different ways. My own funding came primarily from a California Arts Council Artist-in-Residency grant. The Arts Council's residency program funds long-term, in-depth projects not only in prisons but in schools, hospitals, senior centers, mental institutions, halfway houses, and the like. We artists design our projects in collaboration with the staff and clients we serve. Grants are given for twenty-hour-per-week programs that run for a maximum of eleven months of the year and are renewable for up to three years.

Those of us sharing art in prison, or any other social institution, join an existing cultural community. There has always been art in prison, and there are images and ways of rendering these images that are understood and respected by community members. As teaching artists, we honor the culture we visit, and we also teach: share the fine arts skills and attitudes we ourselves have been given.

Of course, libraries contain dozens of books written by men and women who served time in prison without the benefit of formal prison art programs. There are books by Dostoevsky, O. Henry, Martin Luther King, Jr., Emma Goldman, Jacobo Timerman, Thoreau, Daniel Berrigan, Miguel Piñero, Etheridge Knight, Irina Ratushinskaya, and Nelson Algren, to name just a few.

Dostoevsky didn't need Arts-in-Corrections. Others, though—people on the suffering end of most economic and social scales—have grown up believing that what they have to say is unimportant or will not be valued. In order for speech to occur, a person must not only recognize his or her own unique voice and particular thoughts and feelings, but also believe that he or she has the right to express these perceptions. Programs such as Arts-in-Corrections can encourage this recognition.

For twenty-five years I have been privileged to share poetry with previously silenced people. My students have primarily been those whose voices are ignored or excluded from our larger social conversations. When working with young children, or prisoners, or youth at high risk, my job has been to encourage people to speak, and then to listen as well as I can. Such listening functions as a mirror in which my students are able to see a creative, healthy, and wise image of themselves they may not have previously noticed or had noticed by others. After expression and reflection, our mutual task—my students' and mine—has been to put their work out into the world, demand inclusion, and find room at the table.

There are no real jobs doing the work that I do, no full-time positions with employment security, health care benefits, and retirement plans. But there are profound perks. The primary of these is a "job description" that demands one ask people to shape their deepest vision into word, image, sound, or movement, thus encouraging the birth of creative expression in another human being.

Because those of us sharing drawing or dance or dactyls or drumming with elders, kids, people who are in prison or mentally troubled or suffering from AIDS or near death don't fit into the economic mainstream, we're often seen—we often see ourselves—as marginal and isolated individuals acting on our own. In fact, though, we're part of a field. Bill Cleveland, former manager of Arts-in-Corrections, calls this field "art in other places."

Those of us sharing art in other places are not therapists or social workers; we're practicing artists who know from our own personal experience that making art has the power to heal. We operate from a belief that creating is a human birthright given to us all—not only those able to attend art schools or writing workshops.

This country has never funded, supported, or valued artists in ways much of the rest of the world has. Still—from the Works Progress Administration (WPA—part of FDR's New Deal, which put millions of people, including artists, back to work), to the Comprehensive Employment and Training Act (CETA—operative from 1974 to 1983, with a similar goal of providing employment for out-of-work artists, among others), to state arts councils and programs such as Arts-in-Corrections—we do have a history of paying professional artists to do public work.

In this dollar-driven, bottom-line society, often only what can be counted and measured is valued. As Beth Thielen, former California Arts Council artist-in-residence at the California Institution for Women, said: "There's increasing pressure now to prove that we make a difference, that we lower the recidivism rate. Can you imagine? It's as if artists in hospitals were asked to cure cancer!"

James Gilligan, former director of mental health for Massachusetts prisons, wrote, using words similar to Beth's: "'Condemning' violence is as irrelevant as it would be to 'condemn' heart disease. . . . We have to be willing to look horror in the face if we are ever to understand the causes of the human propensity toward violence well enough to prevent its most destructive manifestations."

We cannot "look horror in the face" if we keep repeating the same stories, based on the same myths, with the same conclusions. This book tells a new story, a story of the humanity shared by us all—convicts, cops, victims of crime, and teaching poets. Inherent to this story is the paradox of exploring such a vision in a place like San Quentin.

The last night I met with my students, Elmo, who had been in our class since the very first session, said, "Now I'm going to give *you* an assignment: Write about these past four years from *your* point of view; tell *your* story; let us know what *you* learned." My response to Elmo's assignment is the book you hold in your hands.

acknowledgments

To the web of people—friends and family—whose love, support, and encouragement make my life, and therefore this book, possible.

To my daughter, Sara Rachel Press, the one who was always there when I came home from San Quentin needing to talk. To Sara, just for being her Moon Girl self.

To my parents, Bob and Edith Tannenbaum, and my sister, Debbie Ingebretsen, for everything, including the money each gave, which allowed me time to write.

To companions during this book-writing journey: To Alison Luterman, Carolyn Miller, Susan Sibbet, and Terry Ehret—the women of the Sunday night writing group—for strong support at the start of this project. To The Anderson Center on the Cannon River in Minnesota, and to Hedgebrook on Puget Sound, for the residencies that allowed me to write a solid draft of the book. To Nancy Lord, Connie Miller, Vivian Rothstein, Lisa Schlesinger, and Susan Scott—writers met during these residencies, each of whom knows how to go deep and how to support others doing the same. To Lisa, once more, for her book and her beauty. To Sally Brady, for many things, among them, accompanying me to the hospital on the island. To Kristen Birchett-Leathers, for caring about these men and for the remarkable meals at Hedgebrook that taught me the deep meaning of nourishment. To Corrine Glesne, who, after reading the manuscript at the Helene Wurlitzer Foundation in Taos, took it as a text to her class at the University of Vermont. To Barbara Schaefer, who painted *Sympathetic Magic #3* at the Wurlitzer in prayer for one of the men in this book.

To the Harber-Schrogins—Maxim, Karen, Jonah, and Julia—who gave me a room in their home for months before, after, and in between residencies. Their generosity allowed me to finish this book while being held by the love of forever-true friends.

To Gail Todd, with whom I've shared so much life in the twenty-nine years since my Sara and her Kim were babies. To Gail, whose poems first showed me I wanted to write poems; to Gail, who knows herself the joys and challenges of writing a book; to Gail, for wanting so much for me.

To Bruce Franklin, for his important work on prison writing and for his generous and consistent support and advice. To Bruce, for suggesting William Frohlich and Northeastern University Press.

To Bill Frohlich, Jill Bahcall, Ann Twombly, and everyone at Northeastern. Special thanks to Sarah Rowley, editorial assistant, for letting me know from the start that she supported my book. To Sarah, for always being just an e-mail away with answers to my endless questions.

To Arts-in-Corrections, the California Arts Council, and the William James Association for making so much good work possible, in prison and elsewhere. To every colleague named and unnamed in these pages.

To the memories of: my great-aunts, Irene Ehrlich and Riva Villard, who each believed in me and expected from me as a writer and woman; Myrna Scott, who wrote no matter what, and whose life showed me that it is possible to keep spirit and compassion alive despite any onslaught of demons; Rojelio Carlos and Larry McInnerney, who deepened my understanding of the purpose of art and who first took me inside prison; Chris Brown, whose voice I still hear and always will treasure.

To Spoon Jackson, who believes in me and this book completely and who tells me in every letter to "write reckless." To Spoon's poems, which encourage my own.

To Elmo Chattman, who was there during every stage of this particular journey, from the years shared at Quentin to celebrating the fact of this book. Elmo read each word I wrote, made sure I got prison right, and offered for my title the title of one of his own poems. His intelligence and fierce honesty inform this book and my life. To the book Elmo will write when he's finally free.

To everyone inside and outside the walls of San Quentin who shared this story with me. A few, but not most, of their names have been changed in the pages that follow.

Selections from the following works were made possible by the kind permission of their respective publishers:

Excerpts from *Waiting for Godot*, by Samuel Beckett, reprinted by permission of Grove/Atlantic, Inc., and Faber and Faber, Ltd.

Excerpt from "The War of Vaslav Nijinksy," from *In the Western Night: Collected Poems 1965-1990* by Frank Bidart, copyright 1990. Reprinted by permission of Farrar, Straus & Giroux.

Excerpt from "in the inner city," copyright 1986 by Lucille Clifton. Reprinted from *good woman: poems and a memoir 1969–1980*, by Lucille Clifton, reprinted by permission of BOA Editions, Ltd.

Excerpt from "Lonesome Valley," new words and musical adaptation by Woody Guthrie, copyright 1963 by TRO, copyright 1977 by Ludlow Music, Inc. Reprinted by permission of Ludlow Music, Inc.

"Some Advice to Those Who Will Serve Time in Prison," from

Poems of Nazim Hikmet, translated by Randy Blasing and Mutlu Konuk. Copyright 1994 by Randy Blasing and Mutlu Konuk. Reprinted by permission of Persea Books, Inc.

Excerpts from poems by Kiva reprinted by permission of the author.

Excerpts from poems by Phavia Kujichagulia, from *Undercover or Overexposed* (A. Wisdom Company), copyright 1989 by Phavia Kujichagulia. Reprinted by permission of the author.

"A National Town Meeting: DC/Divided City," from *Nightline*, April 27, 1989. Used by permission of ABC News.

Excerpt from "Which Side Are You On?" by Florence Reece, copyright 1946 (renewed) by Stormking Music, Inc. All rights reserved. Reprinted by permission of the publisher.

Excerpt from "The Man Watching" by Rainer Maria Rilke, from *News of the Universe: Poems of Twofold Consciousness*, edited by Robert Bly, copyright 1980, 1995 by Robert Bly. Reprinted by permission of Sierra Club Books.

"The Line-Up," from *Parts of Speech* (Confluence Press), copyright 1978 by Joan Swift. Reprinted by permission of the author.

"Her Husband to Himself," from *The Dark Path of Our Names* (Dragon Gate Inc.), copyright 1985 by Joan Swift. Reprinted by permission of the author, Joan Swift, and the publisher, Gwen Head.

"Spoon," from *The Tiger Iris*, copyright 1999 by Joan Swift. Reprinted by permission of BOA Editions, Ltd.

The poems written by the San Quentin poets and quoted in these pages originally appeared in *New Moons and poems in other phases*, edited by Judith Tannenbaum (William James Association's Prison Arts Project, 1986); *In His Own Shoes*, edited by Judith Tannenbaum (Arts-in-Corrections and the California Arts Council, 1986); a chapbook series edited by Judith Tannenbaum (Month of Mondays Press, San Quentin State Prison, 1987) which included *In the Hills and Hollers*, by Carl Blevins; *Leo's Fifth Expression*, by Christopher Brown, I; *Beads of Wax*, by Elmo Chattman, Jr.; *No*

Distance Between Two Points, by Spoon Jackson; and *Nothing But The Real,* by Coties Perry. Also, San Quentin Poets poetry reading, videotaped by Gary Glassman and presented during National Poetry Week in San Francisco, April 1987; San Quentin Poets poetry reading, taped by Wes "Scoop" Nisker and aired on radio station KPFA, December 3, 1987; a broadside series, edited by Judith Tannenbaum (Month of Mondays Press, San Quentin State Prison, 1988); and *The Real Rap: A Message To The Youth,* edited by Judith Tannenbaum (Month of Mondays Press, San Quentin State Prison, 1989). All rights are retained by the individual poets, who have given permission for their work to be reprinted here.

Disguised as a Poem

one

The First
Three Months

The evening air was coastal-California, mid-August cool as I walked into San Quentin. Jim Carlson—the man who put together the art program at this, California's oldest, prison—walked with me down the long path that looked out across the San Francisco Bay. Jim told me about count clearing and chow and Close B's and officer coverage. As we walked toward the castlelike structure ahead, Jim spoke of Max Shack, Four Post, West Block, and Yard Side.

I hugged the poems I'd prepared for the night's class, ready to share the language I loved, and silently repeated the words of this new tongue: *Max Shack, Four Post, West Block, Yard Side.* These spondees sounded with my heart's own two-beat pulsation and became the first entries in a glossary whose meanings would deepen and fill the next four years of my life.

....

"Hi," I greeted Gabriel.
"Not tonight; wish I was."

By the time I caught the pun, three other men had sauntered into the basement classroom and slid their denim-clad bodies against seat backs. For two hundred weeks, we would meet on Mondays in this buried room. At 6:30 that first week, and each week thereafter, I welcomed my students.

Elmo—tall, black, and well muscled—loved the poems of Pablo Neruda and was himself a master of metaphor. Though younger than I by ten years, Elmo recognized what he called my "child of the sixties" sensibilities. He himself had grown up in a beach town north of Los Angeles and had wanted to attend art school in New York City. Elmo watched me walk into San Quentin as though I were a traveler in some foreign land, and he generously shared information he knew I wouldn't find on any of the maps given out by the official tourist office.

The "underground guidebook" Elmo opened for me included stories of his own experience and how this experience shaped the man he'd become. "My father always used to say, 'Better to be dead than mistreated.' I didn't know where he was coming from. I was a kid in California, and he was from Louisiana. I'd pull the tab on a beer and shake my head thinking, *nothing's* worse than being dead. But now I understand," Elmo told me within my first few weeks at the prison.

"One thing George Jackson wrote that I've always found true," Elmo said of the author of *Soledad Brother*, a man killed at San Quentin, "'Prison can make you or break you, but it leaves no man unchanged.' When my little brother and I got here, the first day we came through, we saw a man being killed. I went up to my brother and said, 'Don't ever let that happen to you.' And I asked myself, 'If someone came up to me like that, could I kill him?' And I found yes, yes I could. So I'd already changed."

On that first mid-August Monday Elmo introduced me to the white man seated next to him. Richard's face seemed a screen on which I could watch a lifetime of anger and pain. Richard had never written poems, he told me, but as a reporter with the *San*

Quentin News, he found he liked to write. Elmo, editor of the prison newspaper, suggested, "Why not give poetry a try?"

In the following months, Richard would write poems about "lone souls sitting in the rail station . . ." and other "second hand people." He would write, "I love the old man/His sorrow swells tears in my eyes/As drops of acid they burn my heart/I see through his empty stare/Our parallel lives/Empty/All that's left is our beating heart."

Quick and wiry, Angel sat next to Richard that first night of class. Angel was Latino, but refused to think of himself as a category. Over the months, he would repeatedly warn us about manipulation and an elite based on "material, power, and possession"—the refrain that ran through all of Angel's jeremiads. He demanded, "Who decides what a poem is?" letting us know "I am a poem/The world is a poem/The butterfly is a poem . . . /This poem is a poem/Speaking in tongues is a poem/A rock is a poem/ Shit is a poem/And the corn in it too/is a poem. . . ."

Angel believed in revelation, not creation. When, a few weeks after that first August evening in 1985, Richard told us he would be locked up until at least 1999, Angel said, "No, pretty soon all the prisons will be emptied." Angel's prophecies may have been crazy—and his upcoming release date made both prisoners and staff shake their heads—but I loved his visionary fervor and his "demand," as he wrote in his poem "A Point within a Circle," that "the source/ . . . reveal itself."

Coties—young and sweet natured—grew up in Pacoima, the San Fernando Valley town where I had attended CORE (Congress of Racial Equality) meetings when I was in high school. Coties worried. He worried about his own two children, and he worried about all children, and he worried about his people, black people. How, Coties worried, had the community's traditional looking-out-for-everybody attitude disintegrated into a state where—as he described in a poem—"Few truly care/Society's nightmare/Blind ambition/Insatiable hunger/i got mine Fuck you"?

How, Coties worried in the years I would know him, had drugs become more important than black pride and unity? Coties addressed his worries to "You people/Who stand and watch your next door neighbor/Suffer from hunger . . ." and "You people/ Who preach every Sunday and take your people's/Money to the bank of America on Monday. . . ."

In the years to come, Coties would always be the one to inform me of anyone mentioned on the news doing good work in poor black neighborhoods. "You heard of the Omega Boys Club, Judith? Write and find out. Send them our poems. See if that Joe Marshall will come talk to us."

On that cool August evening, Ali entered the classroom, along with Hakim. Manny walked in. Gabriel waved me toward the empty seat next to his own.

Gabriel's face reflected both his Japanese and Caucasian bloodlines, and, as I soon would discover, his aesthetics were also informed by both traditions. Much of what Gabriel had to say simply would not fit into a tight twenty-line poem, and he experimented with forms that allowed as much space for silence as substance. Gabriel would bring *suzuri, sumi,* and *fude*—ink stone, ink stick, and brushes—to class and sit patiently rubbing the stick of soot and glue onto the stone. He would then dip a brush into the black ink he'd created and pause, centering his attention on the blank sheet of paper before him.

Of these eight men who showed up that first August evening, many would form the core of our class over the following years. That night and thereafter, I found every way that I could to teach these men about themselves as writers of poems. But I was also a student. For I learned from each man's particular qualities and unique ways of surviving in prison more than I could ever have imagined about what it is to be human.

In August 1985, San Quentin was a maximum security prison housing more than three thousand men. Its mission, as had been recently determined by the California Department of Corrections in Sacramento, was to serve as a lockup facility for the statewide prison system. This meant that most of the prisoners at San Quentin were confined to the Security Housing Units (SHU), where they spent an average of twenty-three hours each day in their cells. But some, like my students, were housed among the general population—referred to as mainline. These men were locked in their cells at night, but they were able to attend school or prison job assignments during the day, and classes or other special events in the evenings.

I knew that the crimes for which most of the men at San Quentin—including my students—had been convicted involved serious harm to, or the death of, another human being. Angel's release date was nearing, but the majority of the men in my class were serving life sentences. I assumed, therefore, that most of my students had killed someone else. Over time, I learned this was a simplistic assumption. Some lifers *had* murdered people on the outside. Some of these murders were gang related, others committed during a robbery; some were "crimes of passion." Some men serving life sentences had not been the actual perpetrators, but were instead present at the scene of a murder and convicted of "acting in concert" or "aiding and abetting." Still others had killed another prisoner inside the pen.

Some men claimed "diminished capacity" because they were drunk or on drugs when the crime was committed. Some who were convicted in the 1970s claimed to be political prisoners. Many at San Quentin thought the Vietnam veteran and former Black Panther Elmer "Geronimo" Pratt had been framed by the government because of his political background. As one prison official put it, "If Pratt had done what he was convicted of doing, he'd be out of here by now."

I never asked anyone about his crime, and only a handful of men spoke to me of what had brought them to prison. Elmo was present when his brother spontaneously shot and killed a man. The

DA alleged that the crime was a premeditated murder planned by both brothers. Since Elmo refused to testify against his brother, he was serving a seven-to-life sentence himself. Of all who mentioned their crimes to me, only Coties denied involvement completely.

Although I am an enormously curious person, I only once read a prisoner's file. I felt my job was to meet these men as students and poets. The one common thread running through what I knew about the crimes that had brought my students to prison is that these crimes were committed by very young men. Now those young men were older.

During my first year at the prison, our student-teacher relationships developed on a once-a-week basis in the isolation of our classroom. Although I did not forget that many of these men had caused grave harm to another, for me that single fact did not fully define them. In the cocoon of our classroom, I knew these men as intelligent, enthusiastic, funny, and kind; I liked each man very much. Over the next four years, I would watch how the crucible of prison taught us all—each man and myself—profound and complicated lessons about who we were.

In my late teens and twenties, "split" was the word I'd used for my sense of existence; reality always felt dual to me, this and also that. In a college seminar, the professor asked each student to bring in an object that represented freedom. I brought in two images, side by side. One was a leaping red flower I'd painted, full of a joyful, vibrating energy; the other was a print of Edvard Munch's *The Scream*, with its swirling, panicked horror.

Now San Quentin provided its own weekly reminder of the paradoxical nature of existence. Each Monday evening, as I walked into the prison, I passed the Catholic chapel on my right and Death Row on my left.

The previous year, my teenage daughter, Sara, and I had moved from the northern California coast, where we'd lived for a decade, back to the Bay Area, where she was born. At first, we lived in a house with six other people. After nine months of two rooms down the hall from each other, a wait in line for the bathroom, and half a shelf in the fridge, we'd managed to move into our own small apartment.

The apartment we found was in Albany. Essentially the northwest corner of Berkeley, Albany is its own small town. In the country, we had often lived a mile or two up some dirt road: Just picking up the mail required a fifteen mile round-trip in the car. Now Sara's walk to the high school took barely ten minutes. The post office, library, copy shop, and bank were all within blocks of our apartment. This ability to walk everywhere I needed to go felt almost like a miracle. And I walked through those days conscious of this miracle, watching the amber light of late summer cast shadows on sidewalks and smelling the jasmine that cascaded over neighborhood fences.

When I was in college at UC Berkeley in the 1960s, Albany was a conservative enclave with a John Birch Society's American Opinion bookstore at its main crossroads. Now the tone of the town was changing, and although Sara and I had ended up here by chance, Albany was starting to feel like a home.

Though I could walk most places daily life required, each Monday at five I still had to get into the car to drive a half hour northwest to the prison. Past a bowling alley and car wash and onto the highway. Past the boatyards and refineries of Richmond. A right turn followed by a left, and onto the San Rafael Bridge, which spanned the bay. Mt. Tamalpais in the distance. Four miles of San Rafael Bridge and, up over the last rise, San Quentin ahead, framed by the bridge's vertical bracing. Then the highway veered north and the prison shifted left. San Quentin was stark against a blue sky those end-of-summer late afternoons.

I took the first exit, turned left, drove under the freeway, bent right with the road past rows of pampas grass, and traveled the few short blocks to East Gate. On the hill to the right were old wooden houses that used to be home to prison guards and their families and were now occupied by a variety of folk who lived here and worked elsewhere. A development of condos stretched out to the left, where the bay lapped the shore. The visitor's parking lot lay a short distance downhill and had a spectacular vista of water, beaches, bridges, and lights.

I parked and walked up the hill to the massive double iron gate, which an officer had to swing open and slam shut with each vehicle or pedestrian entering or leaving the prison. Most Monday evenings the guard on duty was a gentle-faced man who lived in the country and wrote poems himself. I waited for him to emerge from the guardhouse, unlatch the gate, swing it back, and let me in. Once through the gate, I'd greet Jim Carlson, who was there to meet me and escort me inside.

All my senses awakened as Jim and I walked the long path toward the prison. Wood-frame houses and stucco buildings lined the street to our right. The hill to our left was covered in ice plant and sloped down to the staff parking lot. As we walked, I looked out at the bay and the three bridges that spanned it; I watched the ferry returning commuters to Larkspur; I watched the city lights just coming on in Marin and San Francisco.

I was hungry for each new sensation and expression—lockdown, rolled up, the hole—and each new piece of information. "Count didn't clear until almost 5:30; class will be late tonight," Jim might say. Or he would tell me the numbers I needed—social security, driver's license, birth date—to get security clearance for a guest artist I wanted to bring in. He explained how to borrow a video monitor so I could show poetry readings on tape, or where to photocopy the poems for the following week's class, or how to check the movement sheet before class to make sure everyone's name was listed. Over and over, with many variations on the theme, Jim told me: "To survive and do a good job working in prison, you have to hold onto what it is you want to do and, at the very same time, let go of all assumptions that you're going to get it done in the way you first planned."

At Scope Gate, another officer checked my name against the gate clearance Jim had prepared as my permission to enter the grounds. Then we would walk through the gate and head straight toward those parapets, turrets, and towers ahead of us.

When we arrived inside Count Gate, Officer Murphy or one of his colleagues would sift through my books and my bags looking for contraband, teasing, "You tell her of our policy about new females being required to date male staff?" or wondering, "Those bozos write any good poems?"

The gate we walked through next had the spikes and grating of some medieval portcullis. We walked a few steps, then a guard in a booth buzzed open the hinged metal gate before us, and we were held for a few moments in the sally port—an enclosure with a gate at each end that was designed so that one gate wouldn't open until the other had shut. After the second gate clicked closed behind us, we faced a heavy black door that required my full weight to open. Once through this door, we were back outside—outside onto the Plaza, outside at twilight with birds singing in the old palm to our right—but inside now, inside the joint.

We walked through the Plaza, which was planted in rose bushes. Calendula bordered the lawn to our left. To our right were three chapels, which served Catholic, Protestant, Jewish, Islamic, and Native American prisoners. On our left was a long, boxy building called the AC—the Adjustment Center, where, I was told by more than one guard, "We send the worst assholes, the worst of the worst." I couldn't see the other housing units, off to our left, but viewed the upper floor of North Block above the AC. The upper floor of North Block housed Death Row.

Straight ahead of us, as we walked, was the Education Building; the words "Hospital 1885" were carved into its stone facade. The current hospital sat at the edge of South Block; this two-story building we walked toward was one of San Quentin's original structures.

To the left of Education was a low-slung bungalow. This is

where we were headed; Arts-in-Corrections classes were held in the basement of this building. But first we stopped at Four Post, a flat-topped rotunda about the size of a garden gazebo, which served as a command post from which officers monitored the movement of inmates. Each Monday I would sit in Four Post waiting for our class to begin.

Through the windows that ran the circumference of the building, I'd watch a guard walk the Balcony—the gun rail above the heavy black door we'd just walked through. I'd watch a "free man," someone like me from the outside, walk onto the Plaza, crossing the red "out of bounds" line painted on concrete that marked the point beyond which prisoners could not step.

Inside Four Post, an officer took calls from the blocks, from Control, and from guards escorting inmates from one place to another. This same officer kept track of the prisoners using the pay phone, making sure that the man on the phone was the man who signed up to use it and that no one talked for longer than his allotted time.

I listened to the staff that sat around Four Post "shootin' the shit," as they put it. I listened to the language, to the rhythms of speech, and to the images the people who worked here made use of: "Everyone wants to get his fuckin' thumb on someone's ass"; "See that white dude? He made up the list"; "He didn't cancel for a reason, he just didn't want traffic"; "What is that comin' at us in that blue jacket?"; "What I do all day, I shuffle paper. Not real work"; "Some yo-yo's been causin' trouble up on Fifth Tier"; "Now whadya gonna do, tough guy?"; "The answer is no; what's the question?"

Sometimes I listened to these folks speak whole poems. "We'd hunt up the coast: Willits, Eureka, Fort Bragg. Whatever was moving. Raccoons we hunted with coon dogs. No possums then. Hard to believe, since they're all over now." Or, "These guys be talkin' 'bout all sorts of stuff: Nicaragua, the Dalai Lama, junk bonds. I gots to stay up. They don't make dumb convicts, not for a long time." Or, "T.M.? I'll tell you about T.M. It makes these guys not care. Take a glance through that window. All these jokers goin' 'Ommmm.' You hear those grunts? And then after, they just don't care about robbin' or rapin'. And, man, I need 'em to care. I got twenty more years on this job. I got to finish *my* sentence. If these dudes stop caring about crime, where will I be? Outta a job. Back in the ghetto myself."

Eventually chow would be over and the men released from the blocks for evening movement. Jim and I and the officers providing coverage for our classes moved across to the bungalow. Officer Weichel took a seat at the desk, ready to check inmates' names against the movement sheet, ready to take their IDs. Through the window behind him I saw a world that I would later learn how to name: the Lower Yard, Industries, H-Unit, the Ranch. And, towering above this man-made enclosure stood Mt. Tamalpais. Beyond it, the sun lowered into the sea, unseen from the spot where I stood, but only a short hike, I knew, down the other side of the mountain.

The men were on their way now, ambling across the Upper Yard, past the checkpoint called Max Shack, and then visible to us in their work shirts and blue denim. I followed Jim down to the basement, where he unlocked the door to my classroom with one of the dozen keys on the chain he always wore on his belt. He let me in, reaching around to release the button lock in the center of the doorknob and giving me piece of advice number seventy-three: "Always make sure the door is unlocked when you're alone with inmates. Make sure an officer on the outside can get in if you need him."

I met my students each week in this windowless classroom two flights down. The top half of the wall along the hallway was glass, so the patrolling officers could always see in. I'd shove the solid wood table toward the center of the room and set eight or nine chairs around it. Cigarette butts snuffed in sand-filled coffee cans, computer talk on the chalkboard, the ceiling with square gaps between acoustical tiles: Maybe I had walked in as a tourist, as Elmo had noticed, but this room was beginning to feel like my second new home.

....

On a Saturday in late September, I entered what was called "the Jewish chapel." This low-ceilinged, rectangular room was used by both the Jewish and Islamic men for services and religious events. The fact that I was Jewish had already been a point of discussion in class. One evening Angel had discoursed on "The Protocols of the Elders of Zion" in his general rant about the powerful, international cabal that he felt controlled all our lives. Two weeks later Coties brought in a poem that featured Jewish shopkeepers exploiting the poor. On both evenings, I breathed deeply. I told Angel not to believe everything he read, advice he gave out so often himself that he was willing, as the men put it, to hear it back at him.

Coties's poem, however, was not easily dismissed. As we talked, Coties described experiences in his neighborhood with greedy Jewish landlords and store owners. I acknowledged the existence of such men and women, but said all the stories I had been told as a child about Jewish history were of a people made victims the world over. The message I took from these stories was that a Jew should always be conscious of discrimination, work hard for justice, and never treat another human being badly.

I said that my Aunty Emma had told me that neither Hebrew nor Yiddish has a word for "charity"; the word encompassing this concept is *tzedaka*, "justice." To establish justice through righteous and compassionate behavior, Aunty Emma taught me, is a duty and is essential to what it is to be a Jew.

I spoke of my grandparents' escape to this country in the early part of this century. I told of my grandmother's arrival in Boston on the Fourth of July. As her boat pulled into the harbor, she heard the detonating fireworks and, family legend has it, wailed, "Are there pogroms in America, too?"

Elmo told us that, although his southern California childhood hadn't exposed him to exploitation by Jewish landlords and merchants, this was a common complaint he had heard when he lived in New York. However, he said, assuming a moderator's even-handed tone, it was a well-documented fact that Jews were actively involved on the front line during the Civil Rights movement.

Gabriel's response to the discussion was to invite me to celebrate the Jewish New Year at San Quentin. Gabriel wasn't Jewish. To the extent that Gabriel identified with any religion, he felt himself to be Buddhist. In class, Gabriel and Angel often spoke up for acknowledging reality as it is, while Elmo and Richard railed against what they felt to be such passive acceptance. "Hey, keep on accepting 'what is,'" Elmo warned Gabriel, "and you'll end up in prison for the rest of your life."

When I had mentioned Gabriel's invitation to Jim, he said, "I wonder if Gabriel's letting you know of a San Quentin event you might want to experience, or if he's asking you out on some kind of date." I wondered, too, but was certainly curious about Rosh Hashanah at San Quentin, so Jim suggested that I attend the service, but that he attend, too. That way, he said, Gabriel wouldn't be able to feel he'd maneuvered me into some kind of private moment.

Now, in the chapel, Gabriel was right at my side. "It's nice to see your legs," he said as he escorted me to the seats he'd been saving. "This is the first time I've seen you in a dress."

I shrugged an "I guess so."

My few weeks at San Quentin had taught me that this culture expected a clever response to an opening line such as Gabriel's. Both prisoners and staff admired skillful verbal fencing. At first it seemed to me that everyone was constantly brilliant, always able to respond with a perfect *bon mot*. Then I saw that much of what I had thought of as original language was instead a series of patterned moves. The "hi/not tonight" exchange, for example, had been repeated each week in class. Stock phrase or no, though, I'd never been good at such quick repartee. I stuttered with the first verbal thrust. That afternoon in the Jewish chapel, I had no witty retort.

My body, too, stuttered. What did Gabriel mean by "It's nice to see your legs"? Was he implying something I should worry about? The intensity of the attention Gabriel focused on me made me nervous. In class he sat at my side or directly across the table from me. Whenever I looked up from a poem I'd just read, there were his dark, unblinking eyes staring straight at me.

For this one afternoon, I decided to hand over to Jim the task of keeping track of Gabriel's intentions. This allowed me to sit in my folding chair—Gabriel on one side, Jim on the other—warmed by the sun-filled, south-facing windows and watch a carrot-topped Israeli put the Torah back into its portable ark while the rabbi talked of atonement.

....

Of the eight men who had shown up for our first class meeting in mid-August, Elmo, Gabriel, Coties, Richard, and Angel remained regulars. Ali and Hakim had been transferred to other prisons, and Manny had decided that he'd rather play piano than write poems. Occasionally there was a fresh face—Glenn and Leo often came to class—but most of these newcomers returned to Monday Night Football. The men were, in prison bureaucratese, "black, white, Hispanic, and other," but it seemed to me that they trusted one another and got along well. Each man brought poems to share, each talked with apparent comfort. Within a very few weeks, we were a group.

In early October, a new man appeared. He was tall and dark and his head was thrown back in what I assumed was prison bravado, shyness, or both. He wore a knit cap and sunglasses that hid half his face. He introduced himself as "Spoon," acknowledged my welcome with a sound between a grunt and a hum, and answered my questions about his interest in the class with a clipped "Don't know."

Even this short interaction seemed an ordeal for the man. Spoon strolled to the back of the room, picking up a chair in each hand as he walked. He placed these chairs and two more into a half-circle and sat down inside it, his back to the wall.

In the fall of 1985, Berkeley Repertory Theatre began work on a production of Jack Henry Abbott's *In the Belly of the Beast*. Abbott had been incarcerated in youth facilities and prison most of his life, and had written to Norman Mailer when the author was working on *Executioner's Song*. Abbott warned that very few people knew much about prisons and offered, if Mailer was interested, to share information about the life of a convict. A correspondence began that was eventually shaped into a book. Mailer and the other New York literati who arranged for the book's publication also engineered Abbott's release from the pen. Abbott was a free person for only six weeks when, as he described the event, he misread the gestures of a man he encountered and stuck a knife into this stranger's heart.

The play's director, Richard E. T. White, asked to come visit San Quentin, and a tour was arranged. White, along with Tony Amendola—who was preparing to play the role of Abbott in the Berkeley Rep production—also attended my class. Many of my students had read Abbott's book and most had heard of his story. In class, Amendola read from the script, and the men talked about how prison shapes one's sense of self. I read from Joe Morse's editorial in the most recent *San Quentin News*: "I fully realize that, if push comes to shove, I ain't got a damn thing coming. I will, however, repeat one of my basic beliefs. Society is going to reap exactly what it sows. Who can honestly expect anything except a negative result from treating a prisoner in a subhuman manner for decade after decade?"

White, Amendola, and I had all assumed that my students, sharing so much of Abbott's experience, would be sympathetic to his narration, but the mood in the room was one of discomfort. One man said that Abbott's sensationalized description of prison life reinforced the stereotype of all prisoners as dangerous killers. Another noted that Abbott's failure on the streets made it more difficult for others locked up to be given a second chance. A third said he'd heard through the grapevine that Abbott was less of a warrior than he painted himself as being.

"The man can write," Elmo said, "and we all know the effect of life in the pen. But here's someone who, after a lifetime of being caught up in the system and suffering the kind of dehumanization and psychological abuse he wrote about so brilliantly, had the great fortune to be delivered from that hellish existence." Elmo continued as if he were composing one of his own *San Quentin News* editorials, "Here's a man who was given a reprieve from his past and a glittering path to a new life, and instead he chose to be nothing more than the animal he proclaimed the 'system' made him."

I myself saw tragedy where Elmo saw weakness and was about to speak, but Elmo had more to say. "My heartfelt belief is that anyone intelligent enough to perceive the 'system' as Abbott did, to know and see and feel and understand the insidious psychological impact of incarceration, also possesses the insight and ability to choose whether or not to become a victim to it, or to take control of and assume full responsibility for who he will become."

As we walked out of the prison, Amendola expressed surprise at both Elmo's intelligence and his disdain for Jack Henry Abbott. Elmo had served eight years on his indeterminate sentence; I assumed that one day he'd again be a free man. He always seemed so sure of himself, always trusted his reactions. I wondered if Elmo—if any of my students—ever worried that prison might eventually wear down his own capacity to be a human being out in the world.

So the next week I brought in a poem by Nazim Hikmet. Hikmet, a political prisoner in Turkey earlier this century, had been told he was in prison "because the workers are reading your poetry."

In "Some Advice to Those Who Will Serve Time in Prison,"
Hikmet wrote:

> *Part of you may live alone inside,*
> *like a stone at the bottom of a well.*
> *But the other part*
> *must be so caught up*
> *in the flurry of the world*
> *that you shiver there inside*
> *when outside, at forty days' distance, a leaf moves.*

Here was a man who wrote from his own experience about feel-
ings I assumed many of my students shared:

> *And, who knows,*
> *The woman you love may no longer love you.*
> *Don't say it's no big thing—*
> *it's like the snapping of a green branch to the man inside*

I read out loud the last lines of the poem:

> *I mean it's not that you can't pass*
> *ten or fifteen years inside*
> *and more even—*
> *you can*
> *as long as the jewel*
> *in the left side of your chest doesn't lose its luster!*

The room was silent for a few moments, then Richard said,
"That's a cold poem."

All the men nodded to confirm Richard's evaluation of the
poem's excellence, but when I asked them to write about what one
can do, even in prison, so that "the jewel in the left side of your
chest doesn't lose its luster," the men slouched, put a few words on
paper, sat back, doodled, and stared into space. My "What's up?

What's wrong?" was met by sulky silence. After more energetic effort from me, Elmo finally said, "Who are you to expect anything real from us? You sail in here with your hippie ways," he continued, "wanting us to open up. You think just your smile and your good-vibe talk are going to lead to some deep sharing? Think again, my friend. What you want is too easy; you have to *earn* closeness from us."

Gabriel, Coties, Angel, and Richard looked down at the floor, at the table's flat surface, at their knees. Spoon sat in the doorway behind his shades, as far away from us as he could get and still be in the room. Elmo, however, shrunk from nothing; he hammered me with his eyes as well as his words: "Who are you? Why are you here?"

My whole body clenched in an attempt not to cry, not yet, not in class, and not on the walk back to the car through Count Gate, where the guard on duty was a notorious tease. Not until I was safely through Scope Gate and alone in the night did I let the tears fall. "How could he?" Indignation bellowed. "I'll *never* go back!" Hurt announced, imagining home and hiding beneath pillows and quilts.

In a voice oozing venom, Revenge spoke to the Elmo I'd placed in my mind: "Maybe you're upset because you don't want to notice how the jewel in the left side of your *own* chest has dulled and become tarnished."

It took my whole drive back home for Indignation, Hurt, and Revenge to each have their say. By the time I parked the car in the garage under our apartment, I was able to breathe deeply and repeat Elmo's questions—"Who are you? Why are you here?"—and hear the simplicity of their inquiry.

I let these questions become a koan that I studied all week. As I taught poetry classes to children through Poets in the Schools, as I laughed with Sara, as I worked on my poems, as I walked through the sycamore leaves October had piled on sidewalks, as I cooked, shopped, and washed floors, I asked myself who I was and why I was at San Quentin.

Who was I? In late October 1985, I was a thirty-eight-year-old woman with a fifteen-year-old daughter I was head-over-heels in love with. My pigeon-toed, knock-kneed body housed a shy and stuttering nature. Despite a secure life filled with support and affection, I felt that I was an outsider.

Who was I? When I was little, I had imaginary friends and a head full of stories. Later, I had book after book to read and be lost in, story after story to create on my own blue-green Olivetti. In my twenties, at a bookstore in Berkeley, when I extended my hand to receive change from a purchase, the clerk took my palm in her own, looked at its mounds and deep lines and exclaimed, "Wow! I've never seen so much imagination!"

Who was I? As a teenager I listened to Bob Dylan, Pete Seeger, Joan Baez, Woody Guthrie, Odetta, Brownie McGhee, and Sonny Terry. I read James Baldwin and Richard Wright and followed the news from Montgomery and Mississippi. I sang "Which Side Are You On?" and "We Shall Overcome."

Who was I? Single mother poet with teenager and cat; shy self with imagination; outsider essence still singing "Which Side Are You On?" Was this the answer Elmo was seeking?

Why was I here? Of course I could not yet know how the path of my life would be shaped by its travel through San Quentin, but I was aware that this leg of the journey had begun over two years before, when I developed readings—of my own poems and those by others—which I presented in towns throughout northern California. In December 1984, I was asked to recite these poems at the prison in Tehachapi. I had no idea what to expect, but I discovered that the prisoners responded as I did to poems: as though they'd received bread, actual matter with the power to nourish.

I was hooked by the response of the men at Tehachapi and came back to the Bay Area wanting more. This desire took me into San Quentin as a guest artist in Floyd Salas's poetry class. As Jim Carlson escorted me out of the prison after that reading, he asked if I'd be interested in returning to teach. Absolutely; you bet.

And now, after two months of Monday night classes, I felt very close to my San Quentin students. I was in awe of Elmo's righteous intelligence, even though I'd just felt its sharp sting. Gabriel's attention often made me uncomfortable, but I appreciated his quiet complexity and helpful nature. What Coties called his "lolligagging style" almost always cheered my heart. I admired Angel's insistence on letting the world simply exist and shared Richard's concern for the lost, lonely souls at the edges of cities. And now there was Spoon, the unknown, sitting silent within his circle of chairs.

I was feeling close, but Elmo had challenged my "hippie ways." "Who are you to expect anything real from us?" he had asked. I'd innocently assumed I had the right to ask each man to delve into his soul and write about how he kept his heart alive while in prison. Elmo had let me know my good vibes and friendly smiles, while pleasant, were too flimsy to support what I'd asked for.

Innocence. I sat in our apartment in my old bentwood rocker and watched a soft, sparse rain fall outside the glass. I thought of Dr. Tussman, my philosophy professor at Cal, who once asked: "If a worker in a factory—not knowing the object his piecework will fit into—makes part of a weapon that is used to kill children in a small village in Vietnam, is that worker innocent? Does ignorance grant innocence?"

I pushed myself to define how I used that word, "innocence": a child's spirit and ability to look with clear sight and an open heart. Such innocence might have been merely a diversion for my students, but I felt it had served them well; innocence had allowed me to be playful, to bring in the lighter air of the outside world. That fresh breeze had been welcome.

The previous Monday, though, Elmo accused me, not of this innocence, but of something like "false innocence." False innocence: pretending I didn't know what by now I should know. It was such false innocence that allowed Tussman's factory worker to avoid recognizing the purpose of his labor. It was all very well, Elmo implied, to talk about soul, to revel in rich language, to debate philosophy. But if I thought I understood anything about their world, I was fooling myself.

Earlier in the month, Coties had brought a poem to class in which he described "West Block/North Block/East Block/South Block" and their "hundreds of cages/one on top of the other/five tiers high." His poem had described a cell's "one faucet white sink/with cold water only/and asbestos and rust around the faucet," and its "three inch thick/pissy mattress/on rusted out squeaky steel springs." This poem was my first glimpse into the daily landscape of my students' lives, for my own eyes had seen little more than the flower-laden Plaza and our basement classroom. I certainly knew nothing about the "racial hatred/sexual animosities/petty jealousies and/diligently plotted schemes of revenge" Coties's poem listed. So I could see Elmo's point: Who was I, ignorant as I was, to ask my students to put their deepest feelings on paper? Who was I to ask them to write of their hearts, there in that classroom with Officer Weichel or one of his colleagues patrolling the hallway and looking in through the glass?

I rose from my rocking chair and went to my desk and wrote words to tell the men that I'd try not to assume I knew anything about their experience (a promise I would, of course, break over and over again during the next four years). But the next week in class, no one wanted to listen to my speech. Angel, the first man in the room, began his usual monologue on conspiracy. One by one the men entered, and when Elmo arrived, to my surprise, he was friendly and warm. I was confused and cautious as I started to speak the words I'd rehearsed. But Coties cut short my stammered speech, saying, "Hey, I've got a poem I've been working on." And soon everyone—everyone except Spoon, who was still stretched out in a chair by the doorway—rested his elbows on the table and looked over Coties's poem. By the time Officer Weichel appeared in the doorway at 9:15 to let us know count would soon clear and that class was now over, I'd nearly forgotten the week's heavy soul-searching and how nervous I'd been earlier, coming down the steps to this classroom.

Now Elmo walked upstairs next to me and said, "You know, in that Hikmet poem, his lines about being 'caught up in the flurry of the world,' about shivering inside when outside a leaf moves? That's good advice. I think about outside every day. Not like some dream to help me forget, but in order *not* to forget, to remember, to make sure I know where I am and that I'm not free. If you once say, 'This place isn't so bad,' they've got you."

I knew this was not casual conversation, that Elmo was telling me something he thought might help me understand. I wanted to hear more, but Richard walked up with a story and Gabriel was soon at my elbow.

"Look." Gabriel was staring at his feet. "I've been practicing a concentration exercise." He raised his left foot and slowly lowered it to the ground. "I try to feel my heel-ball-toe settle. Of course," Gabriel glanced at my face and smiled, "it's not easy to concentrate this way out on the yard."

"See, Judith," Gabriel said, again standing straight, turning solemn, "this is why I think we couldn't talk about that Hikmet poem in class last week. It's like what I'm trying to tell you about the yard. No one can afford to talk about 'the snapping of the green branch' in front of a group of fellow prisoners, although each and every one of us has felt that. Hikmet knows. He warns us, 'Don't say it's no big thing.' He knows that's *exactly* what we'll say to save face out on the yard."

Weichel announced that count had cleared and that he had a long drive home; it was time for the men to get back to their cells. I waved and watched my students turn right and walk toward the cell blocks. They each walked that walk: shoulders thrown back, chest held high, and an "I'll take up as much space as I need to" demeanor.

On that late October Monday night, I watched my students walk that tough walk. I watched them walk past the library on their right, past the mural on their left and toward the Upper Yard, straight ahead. Once they passed Max Shack, though, they disappeared into a dark beyond which, I could not see.

two

Cleansing the Doors
of Perception

"Just want you to see," Elmo smiled slyly, handing me a sheet of paper, "that I do know where Hikmet's coming from."

I looked down and read what Elmo said was the first poem he'd written after coming to prison:

> **Metamorphosis**
> *Hostility*
> *like a garden*
> *grows*
> *rising up*
> *out of the grave in my heart*
> *where I've buried the man*
> *I used to be.*

September's red and gold light had long ago burst into October flame; October's brief heat had cooled in November; then Thanksgiving, Chanukah, Christmas, the New Year. Week after week, on Monday nights after class, I watched my students disappear into that dark beyond Max Shack, and I wondered what seasons and holidays were to men who might spend their whole lives in prison; I pondered what each man might have buried in that grave in his heart.

Around the turn of the year, I discovered an article that had been published ten years before. In it, an Arizona prisoner, Michael Hogan, who'd served seven and one-half years on a fourteen-year sentence for big-time forgery, wrote:

> One of the most common experiences in prison is the gradual numbing of emotion. You can't openly express rage or fear without putting yourself in a position where you are certain to kill, be killed or spend a fantastic amount of time in the Hole.
>
> So even though rage and fear are the "natural" emotions to feel in many prison situations, you suppress them, you "hold your mud," you stay "cool." Your wife leaves, your father dies and there is nothing you can do in the cellblock. There is no acceptable outlet for your grief. . . .
>
> So you do not express your sorrow, your remorse, your grief. You are quiet and cool.
>
> Your sense of alienation grows. As the years go by: Christmas without carols or children or presents, birthdays without a simple card, friends dying from overdose or stab wounds, no privacy, not one fucking minute alone, you cease to feel anything. . . .

When people outside the gates of San Quentin heard words like Hogan's, they often sighed, "Give me a break! Where does this guy get off with his moaning? The ones who've ceased feeling are these creeps' victims; *they're* the ones not getting cards on their birthdays. Matter of fact, they have no more birthdays. These losers you want me to weep for *stole* all the birthdays."

Although I myself did weep for Elmo and Coties, Richard, Angel, Gabriel, Glenn, Leo, and Spoon, I understood why others might not. What I couldn't understand, though, was why these others weren't weeping for us all, for humankind.

They weren't weeping, I supposed, because more and more folks outside the gates of San Quentin didn't see my students—or others like them—*as* humankind. They saw them instead as animals who, therefore, deserved life in a cage.

Before I had walked into that Tehachapi classroom, the word "criminal" had been an abstraction—an image on a TV screen, a sensationalized headline, a statistic, a revolutionary hero in some radical rag. But when these men shook my hand, my skin against each large, sweaty, or insistent palm informed me that I touched an actual person. These handshakes served as the pinch to convince me that these were breathing human beings: one with his long, straight, black hair; one with his wild bush of an Afro; one in the back row wearing his prison-issue clothing as though he sat at some walnut conference table in a three-piece suit; and one whose eyes and lips seemed straight from a Mayan sculpture. And now, at San Quentin, spending Monday nights as I did, I saw that even those of my students who had committed the gravest of crimes were not monsters, but human. I didn't see how we as a society could do any serious thinking about crime if we didn't acknowledge this basic fact.

Walking into and out of San Quentin, I thought: "Human beings have killed other human beings; human beings have locked human beings in cages for life. What does it mean to be human?"

A scene from the movie *Playing for Time* often came to my mind. In the film, a group of women are interned in a concentration camp. One of them refers to the Nazi guards as inhuman beasts. Vanessa Redgrave's character shakes her head: No, they're not beasts; they are human. That is the horror; that's what we have to face. Human beings have done this.

Of course, men at San Quentin knew the truth. As one of them put it, "I'm not a demon. I'm not a behemoth. I'm not a throwback or a Neanderthal. I'm a person." Over and over I heard men remind themselves that they were more than animals locked inside cages.

The injunction I heard repeated most often during my years at the prison was "Never call your cell home; it's not your home. If you come back to a cell that's been ransacked, be glad. Let it remind you: Never get too comfortable here."

"San Quentin is a blight on my drive home," someone wrote in a letter to Marin County's weekly, the *Pacific Sun*. "I don't want the view blocked." When my students heard "fighting words" such as these, they responded in a variety of ways that insisted that they be included in the "family of man." As Coties put it, sweetly, in a poem:

> *Say how ya doing*
> *Outside world?*
> *Do you remember me?*
> *I'm that intricate part*
> *Missing from the whole*
> *The one y'all decided to forget.*

Like Coties, I longed to be able to see "human," whole. I longed for a vision that would allow me to see each of my students next to each individual guard, each warden, each victim of crime, each politician, each voter who was convinced that more prisons was a solution. And me, too; I was part of this circle.

I sensed that what was required for such vision were William Blake's cleansed doors of perception, which allowed one to see "everything . . . as it is, infinite." In early 1986, I pinned a quote by the filmmaker Robert Bresson over my desk, and that tacked sheet of paper stayed within sight for the next three and one-half years: "Accustom the public to divining the whole of which they are given only part. Make people diviners. Make them desire it." I desired it.

As late summer became fall and turned into winter, I frequently thought of Hikmet's warning that too many years *looking* tough might actually *make* one tough. I assumed part of my job was to encourage my students to polish that jewel in the left side of their chests, and to avoid what Michael Hogan described as that "gradual numbing of emotion" that would eventually lead to cessation of feeling.

In his article, though, Hogan referred to his fellow prison poet, Paul Ashley, who had died from stab wounds inflicted out on that Arizona prison yard. Hogan wrote: "He let his guard down— something free world poets, I'm told, do quite regularly but prison poets do only with a terrible sense of the risks involved."

Hogan ended his article by saying that he continued to write as a way to tell other prisoners: "There are choices you still can make. The Man can kill you but he can't stop you from feeling. Only you can do that. He can mess you up but he can't make you hate life or lose your sense of wonder. Only you can do that."

True, I thought, but Hogan—with his seven and one-half years served—had paid enough dues to deliver that message. As Elmo's post-Hikmet questions had forced me to notice, I was free to walk out of San Quentin and drive home each Monday night and, therefore, could not claim quite the same right.

How was I going to encourage my students to polish that jewel and always remember how little I knew about the risks in prison to a lustrous heart? "Do I contradict myself?" Walt Whitman wrote. "Very well then I contradict myself."

Six months at San Quentin had already made it quite clear that I'd do well to increase my capacity for living with such contradiction. Encouraged by words, as I tended to be, I papered the wall over my desk with more quotations. Near Bresson's injunction, I tacked F. Scott Fitzgerald's: "The test of a first-rate intelligence is the ability to hold two opposed ideas in the mind at the same time, and still retain the ability to function." Just to make sure I got the point, I added Keats's definition of negative capability: "when man is capable of being in uncertainties, Mysteries, doubts, without an irritable reaching after fact and reason."

When I left my desk Monday evenings to enter San Quentin,

the concurrence of sensations brushing my body summoned the wisdom these writers urged. As I walked into the most maximum security prison in the state, I flashed my ID card and listened to the sound of gulls over the bay. I waited for the guard to swing the massive gate open, and felt a moist breeze against my cheek. I smelled the diesel from a bus bringing in orange-suited new guys, and looked out on the million-dollar view that letter writer resented the prison for blocking. And each week in class, I'd sit in a room with my students, men I admired and cared for, some of whom were also murderers.

One writer whose double vision I cherished was Czeslaw Milosz. Born in Lithuania in 1911, Milosz had lived through much of the horror the twentieth century had to offer: His own country was occupied by Poland, then by the USSR; he lived through World War II in Nazi-occupied Warsaw; he first served, then broke with, Communist Poland; he spent most of the 1950s in exile. Milosz's poems conveyed both the cruelty he had witnessed and the joy of being a creature with consciousness, alive on this planet, able to witness. I loved his ability to express the limitations of being human, while always speaking up for human existence.

But when I brought in a few of his poems to class, Elmo had arguments to pick with Milosz. Elmo read from "Bobo's Metamorphosis": "How much he envied those who draw a tree with one line!/But metaphor seemed to him something indecent"; and he asked, "Why is this man afraid of the power of language?"

Elmo referred to Carolyn Forché's "The Colonel," pointing out, "When Forché had to describe that bag full of severed human ears the Salvadorian colonel shook in her face, she wrote: 'They were like dried peach halves. There is no other way to say this.' Metaphor was the most accurate description she could find."

"But, Elmo," I argued. "Your own beloved Neruda once wrote: 'The blood of the children ran in the street/like the blood of children.' Even Neruda, metaphor maker extraordinaire, saw a horror so profound, the only way he could convey it was to let the fact stand for itself. He knew comparing the spilled blood of children to anything else would cheapen the truth."

Elmo acknowledged my point, but let me know that his preference was for a poetry of passionate language. Milosz's poetry seemed distanced to Elmo.

"There *is* distance," I replied, "but there's passion, too. That's what I love about Milosz. Look at the couplet that follows the one you quoted: 'He would leave symbols to the proud busy with their causes./By looking he wanted to draw the name from the very thing.' Does that sound like a dispassionate wish to you?"

Elmo certainly understood what I was saying, but he wasn't drawn in by what seemed to him a mental passion. Instead he wanted to be overwhelmed and seduced by the energy of a poem's language. I was attracted to, and distrustful of, both passion and distance, and so treasured Milosz's paradoxical vision.

Astounded at the nerve required even to think the thought, I decided to ask the Nobel Prize–winner—now a Berkeley resident—if he would come to our class as a guest. On the afternoon I planned to call, I flitted around the apartment like a nervous teenager. Like a teenager, I sat on my teenager's bed, needing Sara's "Go ahead, Mom, make the call now" encouragement to dial the number. Milosz answered the phone himself and said yes, he'd visit our class on March 17. All I had to do, then, was to prepare Milosz's security clearance and gate pass, and to pray. I prayed there would be no lockdown on March 17, no students in the hole, and that afternoon count would clear early.

The hole. At one time, that's exactly what it was: a dungeon with neither windows nor lights, where prisoners were confined as punishment. Such forms of punishment were common in American prisons throughout much of our history, and they were in use at San Quentin, in one form or another, as recently as the 1950s. By 1986, though, being thrown in the hole meant being confined to a cell in one of the prison's lockup units.

And count. Three times each day, almost all else at the prison stopped for institutional count. This cell-by-cell check confirmed that all prisoners were present, that none had escaped or been stabbed or left buried in a laundry cart somewhere.

Some men were given permission not to be in their cells, and instead to attend a class, job assignment, visit, self-help group, or special event. If a prisoner received permission to be "outcounted," his name was listed on a "movement sheet" signed by the captain. Guards had to account for all prisoners, whether by seeing their breathing bodies through the bars of their cells, or by noting their faces when taking their IDs and checking these against the movement sheet.

Afternoon count began at four, and depending on how smoothly it went, it took an hour or so to complete. When count had cleared, the men were released from their cells for chow. If all went well, the men listed on the sheet for what was called "6:20 movement" left the dining hall and were walking across the Upper Yard toward the classrooms and chapels by 6:30.

We then had about two hours before evening count began. Depending on their custody level, some students stayed in class until count cleared—most often, around nine thirty. Others, classified as Close B's, had to return to their cells before evening count, therefore missing one-third of each class.

On March 17 there wasn't a lockdown but Elmo, who had planned to interview Milosz for the *San Quentin News*, had been "rolled up"—taken from his cell on main line and put in the hole. And afternoon count had cleared very late.

Under normal circumstances, our class would have been canceled. Jim left Milosz and me at Four Post and walked across the Plaza to convince the captain that this visit from a Nobel Prize–winner was not a normal circumstance. Jim must have been persuasive, for the captain agreed.

We had a long wait, though, before class would begin. Milosz sat at a desk in Four Post going over the material he'd brought to share with the men. He was going to read from an interview with a political prisoner in Uruguay. The man spoke of his effort in prison to recall lines from Homer. He ached to lose himself in literature, and spent most of his time reconstructing in his mind the work he loved, line by line.

I told Milosz that my students said they could not afford to lose themselves. I told him how, when I had declared one task of a poet to be that of attention, my students had laughed. "Judith," Gabriel had said, "if attention is what it takes, then we're all master poets. We *have* to pay minute attention in here. We all notice if the trash can on the Upper Yard has been moved six inches from one day to the next. Our lives may depend on such detail."

Jim nodded and mentioned an inmate who had come to the Arts-in-Corrections office to borrow some brushes to paint with. Jim said, "He came back today, and when he looked at the box on top of the bookcase where the brushes had been, he told me, 'Someone's stolen three brushes.' I climbed up to check and saw, sure enough, three brushes had fallen behind the box."

Officer Weichel walked into Four Post, told us that inmates were just now being released for chow and asked if, while we waited, Milosz would like to see a cell block. I hadn't yet been inside such a unit, so I silently hoped, "Yes, let him say yes," until Milosz said this "yes" out loud.

Weichel walked us to North Block and rang the bell. A disembodied voice responded and, after explanations from Weichel, we heard a key turning on the other, unseen, side of the thick black door. Once inside, we stood in a vestibule with dim light and a high ceiling, its paint peeling.

Weichel led us into the housing block itself, where I saw—as Coties's poem had described—five rows of cells, one on top of another. Bars formed the front wall of each cell. From where we stood, we could see heavy wire mesh placed over these bars. Officer Weichel pointed to this black screening and said, "Officers were always having to do the 'San Quentin Shuffle' to avoid being stuck through the bars by some inmate-manufactured weapon. The mesh makes a stabbing less likely."

North Block was the hole, one of the Security Housing Units (SHUs) where prisoners found guilty of serious disciplinary infractions were sentenced to a term of confinement. Gang activity, assaults, inciting others, manufacturing weapons, and drug charges were among the many reasons a man could end up in a SHU unit such as North Block.

The overripe smells of dinner and sweat filled the space. A man on the third tier yelled out his next move in checkers to his opponent two tiers below. A man on the second tier stood handcuffed, wearing only his shorts, while two guards searched his cell. Some men were singing, some were hooting at me, some were debating the news with others three cells over. Across from the tiers of cells, gun walks jutted into the blocks. Officers sat there or walked, patrolling, looking across into the cells for possible trouble.

The reverberating noise, false light, and moist, dungeon-y odors nearly made me faint. *This* is where we lock up human beings? Public money is being used to create *this*? We expect men spending time in a place like *this* to be capable of being responsible citizens-in-the-world in the future? In the following days I told friends, "We give animals in zoos more space and respect." Milosz's stunned response was, "What does a man do here if he wants to study?"

Milosz described European prisons that had no bars, but solid doors. The primary rule in those prisons, he told us, was silence. What does someone do here if he wants to read, Milosz asked, if he wants to write? Weichel said every man was given earplugs when he entered San Quentin. Milosz and I nodded, as though this were a solution.

We walked back to Four Post, subdued, hardly talking. Once there, the officer told us that the men in my class were just being released and we could go to the classroom to meet them. What with late chow and no Elmo, only five men showed up. In the hour granted us by the captain, Milosz talked about good and evil.

Leo protested, "There's no such thing; good and evil are subjective."

"You say that because you're an American," Milosz nodded. "But to any twentieth-century European, evil is not subjective."

Leo stuck to his position, and Milosz shrugged: He understood this view. Milosz told us about a philosopher friend. When she was little, she asked her father, "Is that tree real or am I only imagining it?" He told her it was real because he saw it and her mother saw it, too. But, the little girl said, maybe they were all imagining the same tree. Her father took her then to a hot stove and said, "If you put your finger in there, it will be real heat." Milosz said, still, she was never completely convinced.

I kept out of the conversation, but Milosz's talk of good and evil certainly caught my attention. Evil, after all, was a word often used to describe these prisoners engaged in debate, many of whom had killed another human being. I had never thought of these men as evil, though. It wasn't that I saw evil in subjective terms, as Milosz said Americans do: I knew if I came upon one man torturing another, I would view the torture as evil.

But my life hadn't led me to come upon torture. Milosz was right: I was an American—a white, middle-class American born to liberal and kind parents. I'd never witnessed bombs falling on my city, or the mass killings of human beings in gas chambers, or a roundup of free people who would be sold as slaves. I'd never experienced rape, kidnapping, child abuse, or a gun held to my head. I'd only once seen a beating, had otherwise barely seen one person's hand raised to hit another. My daughter, the person I loved most in the world, was alive and unharmed. Bigotry seemed evil to me: racism, classism, and sexism were evil. Misuse of power was evil. But I'd never met a person, not even at San Quentin, who was evil and only evil. From what I'd observed so far in life, every human being was capable of doing both good and bad, but no one I knew could be summed up forever by his worst act or best intention.

Milosz declared that if there were no objectivity, everything would be a jumble. He said we need to perceive order and that art, therefore, requires removal and distance. To a room filled with protests, Milosz replied that art was not life; life, unlike art, Milosz argued, requires "moral indignation."

"Removal and distance: What did I tell you?" I imagined Elmo buzzing in my ear.

I silently swatted this buzzing Elmo, angry over his absence from class. I wanted Elmo to be part of this discussion.

Milosz's broad face, his Eastern European–accented English, his language of formal discourse, were all strange to the men in this room. They were honored by Milosz's visit and shook his hand with enormous respect. Still, they left confused.

I walked Milosz out through the Plaza, through Count Gate and Scope Gate and down the long path to East Gate. Above the bay's soft play over rocks, that Mediterranean sound, Milosz asked, "Who is the most intelligent man in the class?" The question caught me by surprise; earlier in the evening, his first question to me—"At what university did you study?"—evoked the same reaction.

Elmo was the one I assumed Milosz would consider the most intelligent, but Elmo had not been in class. I stuttered. Milosz said, "I think that young black man by the doorway." Milosz meant Spoon; he saw the intelligence in Spoon's silent face, even behind shades.

....

For months, Spoon had continued to sit silent. I knew nothing about him but his long, black body, his eyes hidden behind sunglasses, his immobile face. Spoon sat at the edge of Floyd's San Quentin poetry class, too, but Spoon made Floyd nervous. He didn't make me nervous. Although I would have liked to have been able to make him more comfortable, Spoon's perch at the room's farthest reach didn't particularly disturb me. If I weren't teaching this class, I'd probably be the one sitting at its edges.

37

Because he said nothing and showed us no poems, I couldn't tell what Spoon was getting from our class. But week after week he was there in his chair by the door, and I decided that, for the moment, what Spoon took from these Monday nights was his own business.

Then, one night in April, I asked the men to close their eyes and wait for a scene to appear from childhood. I asked them to notice the sensual details. If they found themselves in a room, what colors were its walls? Where was the furniture placed? What smells traveled in from the kitchen? What was their brother saying? What sounds could they hear from the streets?

For the first time, Spoon pulled his chair up to our table and wrote. After everyone had finished, Spoon handed me his poem, and I read the first written words of Spoon's that I'd seen:

> *I see the jack rabbit gracefully*
> *attempting to flee from the slender*
> *greyhound who is right on its*
> *tail. He catches the rabbit and*
> *packs it back and suddenly there's*
> *another rabbit and there's rabbits*
> *everywhere. He catches five or*
> *six rabbits. But never catches his*
> *breath so he has gotten caught along*
> *with the rabbits and ceases to*
> *exist.*

My own earliest memory was of myself at age two and one-half standing in the house my parents and I were about to move into. My father was dismantling a crib and telling me that my baby brother had been born dead. It was September in Los Angeles and hot. The window behind my father faced south, and bright light surrounded his body. As I watched my father's hands and listened to his words, I suddenly experienced "myself" for the first time; for the first time I realized that I was contained in a body.

Before this, my experience must have been global. Even since that moment when awareness of self whooshed into my skin, I have continued to have trouble, as current jargon has it, with "boundaries." So, for example, in the spring of 1986, I often sat at some Bay Area poetry venue sensing my San Quentin students around me. I'd be sitting upstairs at the Cafe Milano listening to Lucille Clifton, and I would hear Elmo praise those words she'd whittled to essence. At Cody's, I'd hover at the edge of a folding chair enjoying Laura Schiff's translations of the Romanian poet Nina Cassian, and suddenly Gabriel would laugh at a poem's ironic turn. When Irina Ratushinskaya—who had been a political prisoner in the Soviet Union—read at Black Oak, all my students crowded around me. We listened together in awe as Ratushinskaya spoke of how she'd written her poems with a sharpened matchstick onto a bar of soap. She memorized each line, then washed her hands, freeing the soap for recording the next poem.

I might feel my whole class accompany me to these readings around town, but I knew that, really, the men were back at San Quentin, most likely locked in their cells for the night. So each Monday I would speak about whoever I'd heard read during the previous week; I'd bring in sample poems; I'd rent videotaped poetry readings. Best of all, though, were actual guest artists. After Milosz, I asked Phavia Kujichagulia to visit our class.

I had first heard Phavia read in San Francisco in late 1985. She climbed the raised platform that served as a stage for that reading, resplendent in dreadlocks and cowry shells. I paid careful attention, sensing Phavia had something important to teach me.

By the time I heard Phavia read, I had been sharing poetry in various settings—public schools, community colleges, art centers, and now prison—for over ten years. From the beginning, I had felt passionately that each student's voice must be heard. I especially wanted to give air-space to the voices society most often shut out. I worried that some student might feel excluded or that her way was wrong, so I made sure to bring in material from as many different cultures, written in as many different styles, and in as great a variety of voices, as possible. I pleaded with students who asked for more rules, "Poetry isn't arithmetic; there isn't just one right answer."

In these years of teaching—first in Mendocino County and now in the Bay Area—I operated from a vague sense that art belongs to everyone and that the gift of creating is a human birthright. But my culturally democratic philosophy was instinctual; experience had not yet made me pay careful, articulate attention to what I naturally felt to be proper pedagogy. And though I sensed that the apparently objective technical information I could give students to help them with their writing in fact applied to only a small portion of world literature, I had spent most of my life in fairly homogenous communities and was not yet aware of the depth and dangers of artistic imperialism.

As a child, I attended schools in which the majority of students were Jewish. (One of the football cheers at Fairfax, my first high school, exhorted: "Abie, Izzie, Moishe, Sam/We're the boys who eat no ham./Grab your *yarmulkes*, hold them tight./Come on, Fairfax, Fight, Fight, Fight!") When we lived on the northern California coast, there were a few children from Pomo, Chicano, African American, and Jewish backgrounds, but the vast majority of the student body at Point Arena Elementary was white and Christian.

Now my experience was changing. Teaching through California Poets in the Schools in the Bay Area, I visited classrooms where students had come from all over the planet. In one—not particularly unusual—Oakland elementary school, the children in the fifth grade class I shared poems with came (the children themselves, not their parents or grandparents) from Nigeria, Ethiopia, Bulgaria, Poland, Mexico, El Salvador, Vietnam, Cambodia, Thailand, Laos, Korea, and China, as well as from a number of different cities in the United States.

The population of U.S. prisons was, increasingly, black and Latino. As Chris, a man soon to join our San Quentin class, would succinctly put it, prison was becoming "apartheid, American style."

So in 1985, I carefully watched Phavia on that makeshift stage, knowing I had a lot to learn about the richness of cultures my students—in public school and prison—had come from.

> *to catch*
> > *to catch*
> > > *to catch*
> > > > *to catch, to* . . .

Phavia began with "Martial Arts," her poem honoring John Coltrane, Erik Dolphy, and other masters of jazz, or—as I first heard Phavia put it—African American classical music.

> *we found out how many Miles*
> *a Cannonball has to travel*
> *to catch*
> > *to catch*
> > > *to catch*
> *a speeding Trane a*
> *Coltrane*
> > *quick like*
> > > *exotic in flight* . . .

I often told my classes that long ago, what we call "poems" were not separate from song or dance. I knew this and said this, but watching Phavia on stage was the first time I saw for myself such a merging of melody, movement, and word.

Phavia's poems often used rhyme, a strong beat, and repetition. Often they had a message, clearly stated. I'd assumed, when any San Quentin student showed me a rhymed, didactic poem, that he was adopting the forms of English verse most of us had been taught in school. I thought that by bringing in examples of free verse, I was expanding my students' sense of poetry's possibilities. Image was at the center of most of the poems I brought to our class; awareness of, and ability to use, image was a great deal of the technical matter we dealt with.

But the brilliance of Phavia's performance made me step back and ask myself a few questions. Maybe my students had not been mimicking some out-of-date English verse, but instead were actively interested in poetic qualities to which I'd given short shrift. That very first night of class, for example, Manny said he was a musician, and that poems were like songs, right? Rhyme, and rhythm, and all? I'd nodded and talked about poetry's roots, but now I wondered if I'd cheated Manny. For I'd hardly mentioned "rhyme, rhythm, and all" in over six months of teaching. I'd never asked Manny to say more about what he meant by the notion of "song." He might have meant the ballads of the British tradition, the *corridos* of his own people, or poem/chants like Phavia's. Manny had long ago drifted away from our class, and now I'd never know because I'd never asked.

That room in San Francisco exploded in all sorts of pleasure and praising as Phavia finished her set. As usual, I felt Elmo, Coties, Gabriel, Spoon—the whole group—whistling, clapping, and stamping their feet at my side. This time the force of their felt presence urged me to approach Phavia and ask her if she'd consider visiting our class at San Quentin.

Most often Jim stayed at the prison on Monday nights until all Arts-in-Corrections classes began. The Monday night I drove Phavia to San Quentin, though, Jim wasn't there and Luis, Jim's prison boss, settled into our classroom to chat with Phavia and me until class began.

I hadn't yet met Luis, a short, squat Chicano with bouncing energy and a quick-paced verbal style. Luis was San Quentin's community resources manager, and his job was both to oversee special programs such as Arts-in-Corrections and to serve as a link to the larger Bay Area community.

Phavia talked of her twin daughters, Taiwo and Kehinde, and

Luis said his wife had given birth to triplets but that one had died when three months old. Gemini was their sign, he told us, the sign of split birth.

Phavia asked if the babies were girls or boys. "Boys," Luis said, "three boys. Mexicans always have boys."

....

> *look*
> *know the strength of my beauty*
> *for i am woman*
> *wife*
> > *mother*
> > > *cook*
> > > *Queen of the Nile*
> *i am the epitome of love*
> *the perpetuation of life*
> *i am a well understood arrogance*
> *i am woman*

Phavia began, after my students had gathered.

> *just wide-eyed innocence*
> *of my ancestors*
> *sent me*
> > *woman*

"I was the ugliest baby," Phavia said in response to curiosity about her name.

The men clicked and groaned in disbelief.

"I was so ugly," Phavia continued, "my mama didn't think this baby was hers. But she was the only woman giving birth that night, so she had to accept the fact: Her baby was ugly.

"My father named me Phavia, 'black beauty,' hoping that naming would turn true."

One man after another called out that it had, it had, but Phavia had hardly been flirting.

43

"And Ku . . . Ju . . . How do you say it?"

"Kujichagulia. Sounds just like it's spelled. Sound out each syllable. *Kujichagulia:* self-determination. I gave myself that one."

I sat toward the back of the room, both caught in the spell Phavia had cast and also observing the nature of this particular magic. I saw men responding as men, appreciating a beautiful woman; I saw poets applauding a powerful sayer-of-poems; I saw incarcerated beings cut away from their roots, nourished by talk of ancestors and gifts from the Creator.

Of course I—woman with all those quotes on her wall—longed for moments exactly like this one, moments in which "the part we were given," as Bresson put it, "divined the whole." Bringing in guests from the outside world fed my own hunger and also seemed one appropriate thing I could do to nurture that jewel in the left side of each student's chest.

Over the next three and one-half years, close to three dozen guest artists would visit our class, many returning a number of times. "Poetry" is how we named what we shared, and, of course, our guests and my students did share poems. But when these guests chose to fully encounter the prisoners, when they were "real" as the men put it, poetry was simply the strong-enough vehicle for this meeting; *meeting* is what we essentially shared.

The moment always arrived—whether I was teaching alone or sharing the evening with a guest artist—when the officer would announce count had cleared and class was now over. We'd all gather our papers, walk up the stairs, and shake hands. I, alone or with a guest, would watch the men turn right on their way to the blocks. In that instant before turning left to walk out of the prison I felt, as more than one visitor put it, like Cinderella: Coaches and ballgowns turned back into pumpkins and rags.

One week I talked to my students about the sensation of severance I felt upstairs after class, and showed them a poem I was working on, trying to capture what I felt. The following Monday, Elmo handed me a poem of his own:

For three hours in that basement room
we are cut off
A million miles away
from your daughter and your cat
A hundred yards from death row.

Elmo described the connection in "Disguised as a Poem" and
then, the parting:

It is always the same
For three hours
you or Phavia or Sharon or Scoop
manage to get close to me
only to be peeled away
like the bark from a young tree
leaving behind a little spot
bare and vulnerable
that does not want to see you go
but will die of exposure
long before you return.

Of course *meeting* could not be only one-sided, and most guest
artists asked the prison poets to read their work as well. By June it
seemed time to compile some of these poems in a small booklet,
and our class spent many summer Monday nights selecting poems
and drawings to include.

Over the years, we would put out two more anthologies, a se-
ries of chapbooks, a set of broadsides, as well as an audio- and
videotape of the men's work. With each project, I would learn
more about typesetting, layout, printing, and other elements of
classy production; with each project I would add to the list of
schools, libraries, poetry centers, and interested individuals re-
ceiving copies of our work. But this was our funky, first little book—
typed, and stapled, and very handmade. Still, I loved the men's po-
ems and felt a strong desire, nearly a demand, that their work be

appreciated by a large outside audience. I somehow felt it reasonable to expect that, with the book's distribution, my students would become a recognized part of the Bay Area poetry scene. I wanted inclusion, wanted my students to claim their rightful place as, in Coties's words, that "intricate part/missing from the whole."

....

In early August, the men looked through poem lines, searching for a good title.

"What about Angel's 'Speaking in poems'?"

"Or Coties's 'I am still a man.'"

"I like Elmo's 'new moons.'"

"We'd need a subtitle."

"You mean like 'and other poems'?"

"Like that, but not that."

There was a short silence before Elmo said, "and poems in other phases."

We considered, then smiled. *New Moons and poems in other phases*, the book from our first year.

three

"Endless Echoes of Steel Kissing Steel"

Another late August Los Angeles scorcher. One year after my first class at San Quentin, I was back for a week in the megalopolis where I'd been raised. Smog screened the hills and hung over the valley and canyons. I walked from Hilgard to the UCLA (University of California at Los Angeles) campus, heat and haze a hood around my head. I was thirty-nine years old, on my way to a conference, but as I entered what I still thought of as the old Bus Ad building, I was a little girl visiting school with her daddy. Once again I was Judy, Bob Tannenbaum's daughter.

My father taught in this brick building until 1960, when the towering new edifice for the Graduate School of Management was completed on the other side of the north parking lot. During the 1950s, once or twice each year I walked into the old Bus Ad building with my father, accompanying him to the world of his work.

At noon on those days, "O Tannenbaum" sounded around campus. The woman who played the chimes at lunchtime worked in Bus Ad. She was one of those I'd smile a shy hello to as my father took me on our morning rounds. In office after office, we greeted his colleagues.

Colleague. I loved the word. *Colleague* might not summon the solid image of "wood-frame house," "warm toast," or "madrone in a field," but for me the word had an aura of people who loved their work and came together with shared purpose and passion to create something larger than they could create on their own.

"O Tannenbaum" was Nancy Taylor's way of welcoming a little girl on her visit to this collegial world. I sat in awe, those UCLA noontimes, stunned both by the magnitude of the event—the melody that carried the silent syllables of my last name traveled through every office window and into each lecture hall on campus—and the small secret: No one else knew why this Christmas song pealed out on a hot summer's day.

Receiving such hidden attention was the perfect gift for the child I was. In my imagination, I could strut across any stage; in my actual body, however, I watched the world from its edges.

In August 1986, the adult woman I'd become picked up her registration packet for the "Art in Other Places" conference I was at UCLA to attend, and walked through wooden doors into a large hall. When I'd been little, I had sat in this same room and imagined myself grown up, in a world like my father's. I had never entered that world, however. For, in truth, I'd always been a loner; I had come of age in the sixties and had a political, as well as a personal, distrust of authority and institutions; I wanted to write. I gave birth to Sara when I was still very young. Instead of a coherent, collegial world, I chose a patchwork, pieced-together existence. In the country, I taught a few junior college extension classes, a few workshops through California Poets in the Schools (CPITS), did an occasional editing job, cleaned houses, and read with little ones at the local free school in trade for firewood.

When Sara and I moved back to the Bay Area, I continued to work in this way. Since late summer 1984, I'd taught classes through CPITS, organized a resource library for the Berkeley school district, interviewed women for a book someone else was writing, cleaned a few houses, and taught each Monday night at San Quentin.

I liked being the "poem lady" at schools, liked being a stranger who came into a classroom for five or ten sessions with a bag full of writing ideas. I liked sharing poems that I loved. I liked providing a mirror in which children could see what was in their hearts and on their minds. But I didn't like feeling I was a rock 'n' roll star, jumping onto one stage after another, having to impress hundreds of students each year.

So when Jim Carlson asked me to think about applying for a California Arts Council residency grant, I said that I would. These grants, Jim told me, allowed professional artists to design a twenty-hours-per-week, eleven months-per-year program, for a maximum of three years, at a school, prison, hospital, senior center, drug treatment facility, or the like.

Since Sara and I were used to getting by on very little money, the assured income was nearly enough for us to live on, which was very attractive. Even more appealing was the chance to create a whole poetry program at San Quentin. Jim and I designed a week's work that included the Monday night class, an afternoon studio class he and I would coteach, individual consultations with my students, and a few hours in the lockup units teaching poetry cell to cell.

What attracted me most, though, was the Art Council's description of its residency program as "long-term, in-depth." I'd taken Elmo's injunction—"You have to *earn* closeness from us"—as my prayer. "Long-term, in-depth" would give me the chance to put prayer into practice. I wrote the proposal and in June was told I'd been awarded the grant. When I left LA at the end of this conference, I'd be returning to the Bay Area to begin teaching twenty hours each week at the prison.

On that hot August day at UCLA, I sat in the hall I'd sat in as a child and listened to Bill Cleveland, manager of Arts-in-Corrections, give the opening talk. Bill spoke about how those of us teaching art to housebound elders, runaway youth, or recent immigrants gathered at a cultural center were not creating an art community, but joining an existing one. He urged us to notice and respect the aesthetics and cultural values both of our clients and of staff.

Paul Minicucci, assistant to the state legislature's Joint Committee on the Arts, said that legislators in California weren't pitting art *against* social services but, instead, valued art *as* social service. He said that making art, by its nature, was a force for healing and power. For three days I listened to Joe Bruchac, Grady Hillman, Laurie Meadoff, Liz Lerman, Rebecca Rice, Judy Baca—people who had been doing this "art in other places" work for years.

In line one evening, waiting for dinner, the woman beside me asked, "And what do you do?"

"I teach poetry at San Quentin," I replied.

"Prison? Oh, I could never do that!"

I asked her where she worked, and she told me she taught painting to children dying of cancer. The man behind us shook his head, "That must tear you apart." She nodded, began to say more, but instead asked what brought him to the conference.

"I make theater with old folks. We base the work on stories from their lives."

All around us, people spoke up:

"I dance with schizophrenic adolescents."

"I create murals with neighbors in South Central."

"I make music with invalids shut in their homes."

On that hot evening in August, I stood outside the old Bus Ad building of my childhood, surrounded by strangers who were, I realized, actually colleagues.

....

Back at San Quentin, I walked toward the Education building, fanning myself with the papers I carried. It was midafternoon on another hot day, one of the few by the bay that matched any "inlander's" notion of summer. Spoon sat in the spiral staircase in front of the building, so silent behind his shades that I almost walked right by him.

"Ninety degrees hotter, I'd be warm," Spoon proclaimed as he fell into step beside me.

I turned, surprised, not only that anyone would wish for additional heat, but at the longest string of words I'd yet heard Spoon unravel.

On this Wednesday in early September, I'd just begun work under the grant. Since I'd seen so little of Spoon's work, he was the first student I arranged to meet for an individual consultation.

We waited for the officer on duty to check Spoon's name against the movement sheet, then we walked down the two flights of stairs. "I grew up in the Mohave," Spoon told me as soon as we moved away from the guard, "in a small town. The heart of the high desert. It was the only place I'd been till they brought me here."

I had told Spoon to bring his poems for us to go over, but truthfully, I assumed he had none but the two or three I'd already seen. I was prepared with model poems and information on image and line. I thought I'd have to do all the talking but, in fact, Spoon had plenty to say.

"I'd stand on the main street and look at the mountains that surrounded the town. I thought what those mountains held was the whole world."

We entered the same basement room where our class had gathered for so many Mondays. We'd just walked past the same faded mural, past the same tin cans filled with sand and cigarette butts. The air that we breathed was the same dank, dungeon-y wet, but instead of the mute man I was used to at the edge of the classroom, here was Spoon right beside me with his sunglasses folded on the table before us.

"I was nineteen when I got busted. That same day I'd signed up with the Marines. Wanted to see more of the world."

For months, Spoon to me had meant silence, the shyness we shared. The Spoon who sat next to me now, though, didn't stop talking, and I happily listened.

He took out dozens of sheets of paper from the folder he carried and spread these out on the wooden table, its surface bumpy with carved initials, blemished by cigarette burns. I read lines about wildflowers and sparrows, about deserts and an oasis, about midnight skies and stars that "have no voice yet they're heard . . ." For almost a year Spoon had sat quiet; now, in poem after poem that I read, I was given the gift of Spoon's voice. I loved the language of his long ramble—its rolling rhythms and precise images; even more, I was grateful finally to learn something about this man and his life.

When afternoon count cleared, we climbed the stairs once again. I'd always been drawn to Spoon's silent sensibility, but now I was pulled toward his speech. In these poems he'd just shown me, I saw that Spoon paid attention to everything we talked about in our Monday night class. Spoon hadn't talked, but he'd gone on steadily writing.

Spoon headed toward chow as I walked across the Plaza and out of the prison. The soft breeze of early evening felt like a gift after the day's uncharacteristic heat.

At home I wrote down all I remembered of what Spoon had just told me. The next day I handed him these sheets that I'd titled "Spoon's Words." The following Monday, Spoon handed me "The Heart of the High Desert," the poem he'd created from my transcription. It began:

> Ocean winds
> gentle breezes
> find their way through the bars
> Through the bars
> a sparrow sings
> and its mellifluous melody
> is all about love . . .

. . . .

When I described to people on the outside the work that I did, they often expressed surprise: "*Prisoners* are interested in poetry?"

In fact, though, I met very few men inside San Quentin who didn't create—whether it was poems, paintings, music, woodwork, or some other form of art. "Read and write without rest," Hikmet wrote in "Some Advice to Those Who Will Serve Time in Prison." "And I also advise weaving/and making mirrors." An abundance of time and few other compelling distractions motivated some of these men. For example, many told me they'd begun writing when they were in the hole or on lockdown. "I never thought I'd be able to survive two *days* in lockup, let alone two *years*," one such man said. "But that's when I started to write poems. Gave me a way to get my thoughts out without going crazy."

Some of these prison artists found themselves more curious about creation than they'd expected, and even on main line, they continued to write. Since the grant allowed me to spend more time at the prison, I got to know a few of these writers. Big Ern was one—a large, black, middle-aged man with a full beard and a steady, serious gaze.

"What I try to do is see so right," Big Ern defined the intention behind his writing, "then get what I see down on paper. It's like translation. Within each thing itself are the exact words and rhythms."

I told Big Ern the process he described was one all true writers aim for. He nodded, but needed no validation. "Rebirth. All life must eventually flow through me. My task is to transform the world, to make the gross and the shameful into things of beauty and ascension. I spy divinity."

Big Ern described how he'd developed the attention to see fully. "When I was on Death Row, I ate with a mini-14 pointed over my head. I had to reclaim my mouth. I brought each crumb singly to my saliva. I thought of my mouth as an organ alive; there were my tongue, my teeth, the saliva, the motion of grinding—full taste released in my mouth. If I did it right, there was no separation. Me, all parts of my mouth, the food that entered, all were one, inevitable, the whole truth.

"That's what I want to do in my writing. I know it's all in my head, the way my eyes see, whole. If I can see in this way, what I write will be formed so that there can be no question."

Big Ern often caused prisoners and staff to roll their eyes, as had that now-paroled visionary, Angel. I could see why, but William Blake caused folks to roll their eyes, too. When I talked to Big Ern about Blake, he again nodded. Big Ern wasn't interested in reading other prophetic voices, though; he cared only about cleansing his own doors of perception.

Big Ern was in SQUIRES (San Quentin's Utilization of Inmate Resources, Experiences, and Studies), an inmate group founded in 1967 that conducted a program for kids who were getting in trouble. Teachers or counselors brought these kids to San Quentin on Saturdays, and prisoners took them on a tour, led the kids through a cell block, had them sit alone in a cell, then gathered everyone into a group for discussion. These prisoners, after all, had been the pimps and players the kids most admired. Who better to impart the message: "Look where that life leads: Straight to San Quentin!"?

Big Ern invited me to say a few poems at the upcoming SQUIRES banquet, an annual event—like the Rosh Hashanah service I'd attended a year earlier—where free folk came in from the outside to share a meal and ceremony with prisoners. So on a Sunday evening in mid-September, I stood at a podium in the visiting room, reciting poems.

Big Ern stood next at that lectern. He launched into William Henley's "Invictus," a poem I would learn was on many prisoners' Poetry Top Ten:

> *Out of the night that covers me,*
> *Black as the Pit from pole to pole,*
> *I thank whatever gods may be*
> *For my unconquerable soul*

Big Ern began, moving slowly through the poem's stanzas, clear till the end:

It matters not how strait the gate,
How charged with punishments the scroll,
I am the master of my fate:
I am the captain of my soul!

In late September, I often walked into San Quentin in the morning, and I went to the Arts-in-Corrections office rather than our usual classroom. The office was in the Operations Building, just north of Education. The room's single window looked across the Plaza to the palm tree in front of the Captain's Porch, the building that housed the captain's office and was the hub of all custodial functions. Associate wardens and their secretaries, though, had their offices in Operations, as did the Appeals office and a few inmate clerks.

The Arts-in-Corrections office was, at most, one hundred square feet and contained three desks, two metal file cabinets, a case filled with books, a cluster of musical instruments, a stack of anthologies, guitar strings, videos from the National Institute of Art, drawing paper, boxes of colored pencils, chord books, memo forms, gate clearance forms, U-Save-Em envelopes, one typewriter, and a plant on the window ledge that needed water. When the prison's fire chief passed our door, he shook his head gravely.

Most days, the phone on Jim's desk didn't stop ringing: "I heard Aida's workshop was canceled; that true?" "Jim, this is DeManche. I'm trading with Weichel; I'll cover your classes on Wednesday." "I'm Inmate Dees in H-Unit. How can we get a drawing class going down here?" "Stacy here, Jim. I'm having a problem lending out materials to our band students, and I heard you've come up with a solution that works."

In between phone calls, Charlie came to the door asking to trade an "A" harmonica for an "E." Dale, one of the secretaries and also a sponsor for SQUIRES, stopped by to tell us that SQTV—the prison's internal television station—had filmed the banquet and was going to air my poem recitation over TV in the blocks. Officers flitted in and out, telling us stories about this one who wasn't "wrapped too tight," and that one who was "serious as a heart attack." Pat, another of the Operations secretaries, who had the task of serving as witness at inmate weddings, fumed in the hallway outside our door: "Damn right I'm late! The bride forgot to take the blood test, and I was left waiting for another marriage that didn't take place." Weichel came in with a question about the night's movement sheet and he told us, "Yesterday a female chorus came in to sing at the Protestant chapel, and every inmate on the yard went to hear them." Weichel laughed, "I swear all those bozos were Catholic last Sunday!"

Lynnelle sat at her desk, trying to organize slides of her students' work and enjoying the show parading around us. Lynnelle had been at San Quentin for ten years, first teaching art classes through the Education Department on main line, and now working with the men on Death Row. For many lonely years, Lynnelle *was* San Quentin's art program. Her hair was cut short, and she looked like a pixie, but Lynnelle had earned her black belt in aikido as a sixtieth birthday present to herself.

By midafternoon, Aida arrived to photocopy arrangements for her band class and Sara bounced in to teach Jim another juggling trick before trying it on her students.

As Jim and I prepared to leave the office to coteach our Monday afternoon class (a workshop that combined words and visual images), Peter walked in rolling a shopping cart filled with art books. Peter helped Lynnelle on the Row and soon would teach his own art class on main line. "Whew!" Peter exclaimed, indicating the crammed cart. "I wouldn't say it out loud, but every time I see a bag lady in the city, I think 'Honey, I know just how you feel!'"

On our way out of Operations, Jim stopped at Henry Tabash's office to ask the associate warden a question about the wording on a proposal for an animation project Jim was preparing. Tabash listened, made a suggestion, and responded to Jim's thanks with, "Well, you haven't burned us yet."

"I've made an awful lot of trips to Henry's office, just asking questions," Jim said as we walked from Operations to Education. I had certainly noticed that Jim approached Henry and others he considered allies—folks whose judgment he trusted and who were supportive of Arts-in-Corrections—with a bit of a dumb show. "Excuse my ignorance," Jim might begin, sounding like a befuddled Lieutenant Columbo. As with Columbo's raggedy trench coat, Jim's nonthreatening presence gained him information, and he used this information to make Arts-in-Corrections' proposals successful.

I had to earn respect from my students; Jim had to prove himself to San Quentin's staff. Elmo had let me know that while my smiles were pleasant, any sustenance he and his fellow convicts could rely on had to be sturdier than some easy grin. In the same way, Jim's good intentions would only open bureaucracy's door. Jim had to do exactly what he said he was going to do, on project after project over a long stretch of time, to keep that door from slamming shut.

Elmo, Gabriel, Coties, and Spoon had gathered at the door to Education. At half past three, we all walked downstairs, not to our evening classroom, but to a large room with windows along the west wall. Through the diamond-weave wire embedded in glass, the fall light cast shadows over the tables and across the room's cement floor.

By four o'clock Elmo stood at the etching press creating a card. Gabriel gathered ink onto a brush and, in one stroke, placed a branch of bamboo on rice paper. Coties and I bent over the poem he'd brought to fine-tune, and Spoon sat off in a corner, lost in his writing.

In the late afternoon sun-beginning-to-go-down hour we shared during afternoon outcount, I recited some lines fourth graders had written in poetry classes the previous week. "The streets are loud/ like a drum beating"; "I can taste the wind as it blows by"; "The corn leaves looked like scary hands in the forest."

Spoon took the poems from my hands, hungry to study the way youngsters described the world that they saw. Jim gave Elmo some advice at the press, and I listened to what moved through the room, that sensation I loved, the force of connection.

Then Jim swung this mood on a sharp right turn, posing a riddle. "Why was the little shoe crying?" Jim asked.

"Because it caught its tongue?" Gabriel replied.

"No, but that's pretty good." Jim paused to wait for any more guesses, then gave us the answer. "Because its mommy was a sneaker and its daddy was a loafer."

Gabriel grabbed his stomach and Elmo shook his head saying, "Jim, I'm worried about you."

The sky behind Mt. Tamalpais reddened. Coties sat in front of the room's metal-in-glass windows and read out loud the poem he'd just finished.

By five o'clock, the men left for chow and Jim and I were on our way to the staff snack bar. This good-bye was easy, though, for we knew—unless some prison drama exploded—that we'd reconvene in an hour or so for Monday night class.

....

"One of the awful things when I worked here alone," Lynnelle said as we walked from Operations past Four Post, "was that nobody but me saw the artwork. When I see something beautiful, I want other people to see it, too." I followed Lynnelle into Education and to the closet where she stored the supplies that she took to the Row. I'd asked if I could watch her teach, in preparation for the cell-to-cell teaching I was scheduled to begin soon in lockup.

In September 1986, there were just over two hundred men on Death Row. North Seg—where the condemned had been housed—did not have enough cells for such numbers, so the Row had been extended to the top tiers of C Section, where Lynnelle and I were now headed.

Lynnelle's first group of lockup students were housed in AC, the

Adjustment Center, the building on our left as we entered the Plaza each day. Lynnelle had designed a cart with compartments for paper, paint, pencils, and magazines; it was easy, she told me, to maneuver the cart through AC's big stairways. When she began work with the condemned in North Seg, there was an elevator she could drag her cart onto. In C Section, though, she said, there was neither walkway nor elevator, only a ladderlike metal staircase that ascended at an angle from the ground floor to the fifth tier. So in C Section, Lynnelle hauled her supplies in various bags she slung over her shoulders.

Together we packed up these bags with material enough for the ten men we planned to see. As we shouldered the bags past Max Shack, onto the Upper Yard, over to South Block and into C Section, I gave thanks that I—twenty-five years younger than Lynnelle—was a poet needing only paper and pencil.

Inside the unit, Lynnelle showed me where the puncture-resistant vests were kept and how to fit the lining into the heavy outer casing. The sergeant in charge wanted us to wear these "turtle shells," though with one on, I moved as ponderously as that reptile did beneath its armored weight.

We carried our bags up that long staircase. The concrete floor beneath us was littered with paper and styrofoam containers that earlier must have held breakfast. Now, as we stood at the locked gate to the third tier, I watched the officer distributing lunch. He pushed a metal cart filled with sacks, stopping at each cell and unlocking a narrow rectangular food port, slipping the lunch in, then locking the door to the food port again. Eventually the officer made his way down the tier to the gate, which he unlocked. "Ladies," he said with a slight bow.

As I followed Lynnelle to the end of the tier, I glanced into the cells that we passed. Centerfold bodies were taped to some walls, a short piece of rope hung from many bars, and one man sat on the toilet at the back of his cell. I averted my eyes to give this man whatever privacy there might be, and looked, instead, across from the tier at the gun rail on which an armed guard patrolled.

I smelled fire, something singed, then saw a man bring a cigarette to one of those short lengths of hanging rope. As he inhaled I saw that one end of the rope had been lit and so served as an ever-ready cigarette lighter.

Lynnelle stopped at Cell Number Two and introduced me to Steven. He had clearly been expecting this visit and was prepared to show Lynnelle the work he'd done since she was last there. The bars in C Section were covered with that same diamond-patterned black metal screen I'd noticed in North Block. Trying to see Steven's painting was like looking at one of those perception tests, where first you see an old woman's haggard face and, after blinking, you see instead a young woman in a hat. Blink: I saw Steven's painting of a man on the yard. Blink: I saw black metal.

We moved down the tier, stopping only at Lynnelle's students' cells, although many men called out to us. After an hour, I was completely exhausted: There were the bags that we carried, the heavy vests that we wore, the risen heat in the block, the constant noise, the effort to look at each man and his work through the di-amond-patterned screen between us. Beyond these physical bur-dens, though, was the exertion of keeping myself focused on what I was there to learn from Lynnelle while desperation pulled me be-low the surface. For walking through lockup brought me back to my own days locked up, though the small mental hospital I'd spent a brief time in was plusher by far than North Block or C Section.

In 1964 I was seventeen, barely three months into my first se-mester at the University of California at Berkeley. Fall 1964 at Cal was the Free Speech semester. My response to the profound cul-tural shift I was part of—as well as to my own personal experiences of intellectual excitement, sexual initiation, and life in a boarding-house filled with dozens of intense young women—was to fall apart. Imagination, my ally, now wildly galloped. I was no longer "making up stories"; instead, narrative ran amuck and disconnect-

ed images and phrases bombarded me constantly. The only re-
sponse I could summon to manic highs followed by swift and steep
plummets was to try to kill myself.

Walking through C Section with Lynnelle called forth memo-
ries of the mental hospital I stayed in after that suicide attempt.
These memories were filled with keys and locks and rules and the
consequences of breaking rules. Primarily, though, my memories
were of other people, with their own definitions of sanity, having
control over my life.

One evening toward the end of my stay, for example, I felt real-
ly well. I felt so well I started doing *grandes jetées* down the hospi-
tal's long corridor. From every doorway came the women on my
unit. "Stop!" each one warned me. Leaping down the hallway
would prevent my release, they counseled: Never show any spirit
in here. I was shocked that the happiness and liveliness I finally felt
after weeks of deadened despair could be perceived by the au-
thorities as a problem and work against me. Still, I trusted these
women's hospital knowledge and stopped dancing.

After I left, a doctor I'd talked to for no more than five minutes
each morning—and these talks dealt only with questions about
medication—called my father to say that I was clearly schizo-
phrenic and would never be able to live a normal existence. Luck-
ily for me, my parents were knowledgeable and self-confident
enough to trust their judgment rather than the words of this "ex-
pert." But this experience, like that of the *grandes jetées* down the
hospital hallway, intensified my wariness around anyone who had
the power to control my life. It was simple: If I had had different
parents, this doctor and his based-on-no-information diagnosis
might have had me locked up in back wards forever. Which side
was I on? I was on the side of anyone at the mercy of the Powers
That Be.

Now in C Section, the Judith who had been labeled schizophrenic
and counseled against stag leaps down the hallway felt pulled to
each man we walked past. I'd asked Lynnelle to join her before I

began my own cell-to-cell teaching so I could learn from a pro I respected. I wanted to see how she managed to balance offering art and honoring maximum security needs in a setting both more intimate and demanding than my classroom. Knowing how to assemble those turtle-shell vests and which officer to ask what of might give me a bit of familiarity with this fantastically unfamiliar world.

What I hadn't expected was how much Lynnelle's work depended on precise pacing. As she moved from one cell to another, she encountered man after man locked up nearly every hour of every day; man after man for whom she was likely to be the only person at San Quentin interested in the thoughts, feelings, and sensations explored in his art; man after man sentenced to death in our names. Each man lived with the harm he had caused and the gun to his temple; each man's need for human warmth and compassion must have been unending.

Lynnelle's time, though, was not unending. She had three hours to see ten men—to look at their artwork, make comments, hand out materials and supplies: eighteen minutes per man.

When I admired her ability to give of herself in measured doses, Lynnelle told me, "It's taken ten years of practice. When I first went up, I'd get caught. I'd always stay too long. But I realized that if I kept that up, I'd burn out in a year. And I wanted to be here for the long haul."

I did, too, but I didn't know if I could learn how to keep walking from one man's cell to the next, smiling and friendly, while inside I was sinking, about to drown. I realized, of course, a similarly impossible task was required of the men of San Quentin 24/7, as they put it.

It was midafternoon by the time Lynnelle and I returned to Education to empty those bags we still carried. The main line inmates' workday was over, and there were still a few minutes before they had to return to their cells for four o'clock count. Spoon sat in that spiral staircase he seemed to have claimed. When he saw us approach, he stood up and was soon at my side, handing me a sheet of paper. I took the sheet but kept on moving, en route to that closet where Lynnelle stored her supplies.

After the bags were unloaded and the closet door locked, I took Spoon's paper out of my pocket, and unfolded and read it. A poem.

No Beauty in Cell Bars
Restless, unable to sleep
Keys, bars, guns being racked
Year after year
Endless echoes
of steel kissing steel
Noise
Constant yelling
Nothing said
Vegetating faces, lost faces
dusted faces
A lifer
A dreamer
Tomorrow's a dream
Yesterday's a memory
Both a passing of a cloud

How I long
for the silence of a raindrop
falling gently to earth
The magnificence of a rose
blooming into its many hues
of color
The brilliance of a rainbow
when it sweetly lights up the sky
after a pounding rainfall . . .

Spoon's poem continued, ending with that line he'd chosen as title, the one that summed up the three hours I'd just lived through and the memories those hours summoned: "There's no beauty in cell bars."

"Listen to this," I said to Lynnelle, remembering that just that noon she had told me how awful she'd felt when she worked at the prison alone, with no one to appreciate the artwork her students were making. Lynnelle listened and stood still, helping me hold all I was feeling: birth, that at this moment I witnessed a birth.

I went out to find Spoon, who sat again inside the staircase. I wasn't crying, exactly, as I spoke to Spoon, but the bones that circled my eyes were throbbing, and the sockets themselves felt filled.

four

"You Gotta Walk That Lonesome Valley . . . "

I stood outside a latticed black metal gateway. The arched entrance was twice as tall as I was and many times as wide. I was alone in this courtyard under a blue November sky, trying to remember how Jim got the guard's attention when we were been here on Monday. "Ah, excuse me," I rattled the gate. "Is anyone there?"

I shifted the weight of the bundle I carried, then repeated my timid call. A man in olive green pants and shirt finally saw me and laughed, "You'll have to yell louder than that if you want to be heard in this zoo. Hold on, I'll go get Smitty; he's the one with the keys."

I slid my ID card toward Officer Smith through an opening between the metal slats. I told him I was there to see my students, bring them some papers, and look at their poems.

Officer Smith found the right key on the heavy chain he lifted from where it rested against his hip and opened the human-sized door in that giant-sized grillwork. I showed him the newsprint stacked in my arms. He shrugged, barely checking the material, and said, "I got no problem with that."

I walked into West Block and toward the metal staircase that switchbacked up to each of five tiers. Each tier held one hundred cells. As I climbed, I heard men calling back and forth, one to another:

"I should've told her . . . "

"Yeah, Homes, I know how it is."

"You sure that's your move? Looks like my pawn's *bound* to take your knight."

"I gots property; I don't need the police comin' into my cell."

West Block was this noisy in the early afternoon because San Quentin had been on a lockdown for more than one week. In the fifteen months I'd been at the prison, there had been many lockdowns for a variety of reasons: a slashing assault in West Block; a stabbing on the yard; a fight between two Hispanics that led to the discovery of weapons that the officers called "shanks" and prisoners referred to as a "flat," "piece," "*keisu*," or "*fillero*." "Inmate manufactured stabbing instrument" was the term used in the formal reports. In each case, the main line population, or some part of it—Hispanics in the latter incident; blacks, whites, or the men classified as "other" in different altercations—would be closed down, all the men locked in their four-and-one-half-by-eleven-foot cells.

Often the incident that precipitated a lockdown resulted from the betrayal of the code by which convicts lived. According to this code, as it was explained to me, every prisoner was expected to conduct himself in a particular manner: to pay his debts, to show each man due respect, to mind his own business, and never to snitch—not on anyone, not about anything. Prisoners felt such a code was necessary in order to avoid bigger problems, such as racial conflict. If a man of one race disrespected a man of another race by stealing something from his cell, for example, a large-scale racial conflict could result if the victim chose to retaliate personally. So, instead, members of the offending party's own race were expected to discipline the culprit and make sure that proper compensation was made. If such discipline and compensation did not occur, the man who had been offended was obligated to retaliate— usually in the form of an assault—even at the risk of instigating a larger racial conflict. If the man failed to take action, he would lose face in the eyes of his peers, as well as in the view of the prison population at large, and he would surely encounter further victimization. Since the administration was usually unaware of the details behind any altercation, officials locked the whole prison down while they assured themselves that no bigger trouble was lurking, no Mexican Mafia plotting against the Nuestra Familia, no white against black showdown, no riotous hit against staff being planned.

In fact, my work at San Quentin had begun with a lockdown. I'd been contracted to teach starting in early July 1985, but in June Howel Burchfield, a correctional sergeant, had been killed in C Section, and the prison was locked down for much of the summer.

Such a murder was unusual, though I didn't know that. Before I entered San Quentin, the world of prison was so completely foreign to me, I was unable to think about any of its particulars. I felt sad for Burchfield and his family, of course, but it didn't cross my mind to be nervous for myself. Instead, I remained very focused on what I wanted, which was to begin teaching. However, week after week I called Jim, only to be told, "Nope, we're still not able to program."

The present lockdown also looked as though it would last for a while: A black man had been stabbed twenty-six times by three white men. In Operations, staff was saying that the investigation was turning up information that didn't make prison officials any too happy.

I walked up to fifth tier and started on Yard Side, trying to remember everything Jim had told me on Monday when he'd brought me to West Block. "Walk close to the railing, away from the cells," he had warned. "Catch the eye of the officer on the gun rail; make sure he knows you are here."

Small bursts of light flashed at random moments from various cells. "You a counselor?" a man yelled even before I'd passed. I wondered how he had sensed my approach, then saw the hand mirror he held positioned to catch my reflection as I walked down the tier. Beckoning fingers reached out between bars. "I got something to tell you," the man crooned.

Finally, I found Cell Number Thirty. Elmo's long body was stretched out on the cot, his head half under a thin pillow. He startled awake and smiled when he saw me at the bars.

"Hey," he said warmly as he walked toward where I stood. "What time is it?"

"About one," I answered, putting the bundle of papers down on the tier. I picked up single copies of *Poetry Flash* and the *San Francisco Bay Guardian*, rolled these into a long cylinder, and nudged it through the bars of the cell. I noticed that Elmo had created a photo display on the wall across from his cot. There were women and children and couples and families and groupings of friends: all of the folks, I assumed, who loved Elmo.

"During lockdowns, most of us sleep half the day," Elmo said, taking the papers and placing them on his bunk. "Night's the only time you can hear yourself think." He grinned, "It's nice to see your face, Tannenbaum. You got permission to come up here alone, huh?"

I nodded. Before the lockdown, our Monday night class had been gathering poems for our second anthology. Now, with such group work impossible, I had told Jim that I'd like to visit my students cell to cell to work on their poems. If the lockdown was going to go on for as long as rumor estimated it would, I might as well use the time to typeset the poems, paste them up, and have the book printed.

Elmo lifted a sheet of paper from the foot of his cot. "Let me run this one by you," he said.

We stood on opposite sides of the bars as Elmo read me a revised version of "This Hole Where I Live":

I awaken with pig iron fantasies
weighing my thick skull down to this dingy pillow
binding me to thoughts of things
I cannot have
or do
or be
A ball and chain
strapped to my cerebellum
A barbed wire noose
around my brittle neck
Concrete sarcophagus gilded in steel
Good morning world
Please count me among the living . . .

Eyes closed, I saw image after image from Elmo's poem: "The rich iron ore has been extracted/from the earth of my flesh/The strip-mined wounds . . . bleed black blood/liquid onyx/dark as the vision of ten blind men" and "a siren wails inside me/crying out like a child in Cambodia/ignorant of napalm/but knowing it burns the flesh off her body . . ."

How can anyone this brilliant and talented be in prison, I wondered for the hundredth time. The way I saw it, Elmo was a big factor in our class's success. Without calling attention to himself, Elmo had helped create an atmosphere in which students felt relaxed and trusting enough to share their work. He was respected for what he knew, and also for the way he said what he knew. He was quick to see what worked and what could be improved in a poem and was able to deliver this information in a way that allowed each poet to listen and respond. More than one student, shy of sharing his writing, had said to me, "Well, I feel okay about letting you and Elmo see my poems."

Elmo was most often the man guest artists talked of as we left the prison's gates. For Elmo could converse with a book-taught, abstract-thought mind like my own, and then turn around and speak straight with some street-smart someone else.

I'd heard stories from guards about Elmo's anger, but from what I'd seen, this anger looked like a righteous response to situations of stupidity or brutality, or attempts at dehumanization. Elmo was simply smarter than most of us, and I assumed he was disliked by staff because of his intelligence and his willingness to use it. "Just wait and you'll see," I'd been told.

I continued along the tier toward Gabriel's cell, engulfed by the noise of the block. I thought of the Joe Morse editorial in the most recent *San Quentin News:* "After 134 years someone decided there's a ventilation problem in the cell blocks. (Well, at least we can't accuse 'em of making hasty decisions.) The solution? They nailed all the windows shut and installed grain elevator fans. I ain't sure it solved the ventilation problem, but it at least has taught me what it's like to sleep under an airplane which is warming up all four of its engines."

No way did I catch Gabriel asleep. He was waiting for me, his fingers curled round the bars. Gabriel told me he had heard my laugh down the tier, but his immaculate appearance suggested he had somehow prepared for my visit. I'd no idea how, though, since I hadn't known until that morning that the associate warden in charge would give me permission to travel to West Block alone.

Gabriel pulled a box from under his bunk and thumbed through dozens of folders. "These," he said, pointing to the files in front, "hold the poems that I've written. And these," he added, indicating those at the rear, "hold all the poems you've given us to study in class.

"Here." He took a single sheet from the front file and walked back to the bars. "Here's my third poem for the anthology. You read it; I want to hear you read it."

I turned to catch enough light to see Gabriel's words on the page:

> *I wanted to paint rainbows for her*
> *water color rain drops*

splashed upon aged rice paper . . .
yet all she saw was gold . . .

I was stuck, as I frequently was with Gabriel, between respond-
ing to the lushness of his language and acknowledging the mes-
sage he more and more persistently and explicitly tried to hand me
about his love for me. As usual, I felt trapped, and Gabriel was
right, as he said in this poem; instead of speaking of "the heart
which held clay," I "spoke of what could fill it." I spoke of the
poem, its intensity of feeling, its rich rhythms, imagery, and sound.

"This is gorgeous, Gabriel. The music of these lines—'Hues my
heart bled,' 'slowly spun with tender hands.' I love these 'short-
lipped snapdragons.' I wonder, though, here in the third stanza . . ."

"I can't hear you," Gabriel said, moving closer to his side of the
bars.

Automatically I stepped back. I hated this response because, re-
ally, I liked Gabriel, liked all the ways in which he was a kind, car-
ing, thoughtful human being. Besides, I knew about love—knew
both about the gift of a love that had saved my life and, also, about
unmatched longing.

Even after I was released from that mental hospital when I was
seventeen, I continued to be pitched back and forth between the
poles of frenetic anxiety and dense depression. Then, just after my
eighteenth birthday, I met Ronnie, and we fell in love and soon
shaped a life: I returned to school in Berkeley, we married, I gave
birth to Sara, we built our own home in the country one-quarter
mile from the sea. Ronnie's love gave me strength and support, and
the good life we made together provided a structure within which
I felt safe.

By my thirty-third birthday, though, this safety felt stifling. For
months I'd been hearing a voice urging me to go deeper, to step
out from under protection. I didn't blame Ronnie for what I was
feeling, but these feelings made no sense to him. Ronnie was so
used to my ups and downs, he reasonably assumed I was just on

one of my usual roller-coaster rides. But, although I was surrounded by fog and once again hearing voices, I didn't feel afraid, as I had when I was seventeen. Now, though my world seemed to be crumbling, I felt curious and excited. After fifteen years, I was again being tossed on tides I could not control. And instead of fear, I felt something like faith.

I did leave my marriage. Then I sold everything I owned and wandered through Europe. I hitchhiked, Magic Bussed, dug potatoes on a tiny island off the west coast of Scotland, served Christmas dinner in a hotel south of London, and shared a single room with Sara—who, at age ten, flew over alone to meet me—in Paradou, a small village in Provence. There I did housework and taught "Five Little Monkeys" and "Itsy Bitsy Spider" to the little kids in Paradou's two-room schoolhouse while Sara studied in French with the older kids next-door.

When Sara and I returned home, I became lovers with Nicholas. If Ronnie had been a life preserver lovingly keeping me afloat, Nicholas was a constantly repeating recording of the Stones, singing "You can't always get what you want."

"Puppy dog love," Elmo called the attention Gabriel showed me. But I remembered my own feelings of longing as an obsession; I spent months scanning Nicholas's gestures and sifting through his words for any slight sign of a shift in his heart. Gabriel now applied this same scanning and sifting to me.

In November 1982—exactly four years before this visit to West Block—Nicholas fell in love with someone else, and suddenly, there were no more gestures to scan. All the signs shone precise and in neon: dead end.

That November I'd just moved from two rooms on a bluff, where I'd lived with Sara, to a hand-built cabin surrounded by woods. In this tiny house, without electricity or toilet, my most constant companions were the carpenter ants that fell from the rafters and the field mice that ran through the kitchen at night.

"For among these winters there is one so endlessly winter/that only by wintering through it will your heart survive," Rilke wrote in *Sonnets to Orpheus*. The winter of '82–'83 *was* endlessly winter. In cabins all along the north coast that winter, people joked that we had finally beaten Noah's record for rainfall. We dashed into town when the sky cleared to grab a gallon of milk from Gilmore's or run into the post office to pick up our mail, but we'd hurry back up rutted roads hoping to return to our cabins before the next downpour. Sara was with her dad a few miles south, and I lived with the carpenter ants, lonely and sad.

And sadness spread from the simple loss of one man to the recognition of the full truth of my aloneness. In London I had received a letter from Barbara, my close friend since high school. She wrote in response to how flippant I had apparently been in writing to her about lovers in Europe. Barbara warned: "You act as though you'll go through this stage and then it will be over; you'd better realize *this is your life*." When I read her words then, I had actually shivered; now that chill seeped deep in my bones.

"You gotta walk that lonesome valley/You gotta walk it by yourself./Nobody here can walk it for you/You gotta walk it by yourself."* I'd sung these words along with Woody Guthrie for more than half my life. But, now, at age thirty-five, I realized just how painful such a solitary journey could be. This pain was like the pain of migraine: The only way to tolerate its insistent presence was to surrender, to relax into the throbbing, to enter the precise center of ache. Wherever I moved, the pain was still there, so I finally stopped moving. Then this settling, occasioned by enormous distress, became something like peaceful, became that going deeper I'd been urged toward in leaving my marriage, became touching the earth.

And poems became part of this grounding. In *News of the Universe*, the one book I'd lugged around in my backpack through Eu-

*From Woody Guthrie's adaptation of "Lonesome Valley," © 1963 (renewed) by TRO and 1977 by Ludlow Music, Inc., New York. Used by permission.

rope, Robert Bly wrote about the Japanese concept of *mono no aware*, which he translated as "the slender sadness." The tone of nature is grief, Bly wrote. On nights between rainstorms, that wet north coast winter, I'd walk an old logging road that circled the cabin, saying poems out loud. My feet in their Wellies, I slushed through puddles memorizing poems. "After great pain, a formal feeling comes . . . " I started with this one by Emily Dickinson, and then memorized dozens more. Days on which the van that served as the county's single bus line traveled, I'd take it up coast to set poems in lead type and print them on an old Chandler & Price: Mary Oliver in Caslon, James Wright in Goudy Old Style.

By this time, I had been reading, writing, and teaching poetry for many years. But now the steady rain, my hurting heart, and the solitude of a small cabin whose windows looked out on thick stands of fir forced a quiet and stillness that allowed me to sink to the depths of the poems that I loved. That relentless wet winter I learned what it means to have poems by heart.

I couldn't give Gabriel a cabin or forest or the love that he wanted. But I could give the poems that perhaps for him, as for me, might be a strong enough vessel for passage through pain.

As I walked past the rear staircase and over to Bay Side, I watched the murky light fall through those high-vaulted but quite dirty windows that rose more than half of West Block's height. On Bay Side, wind and the calling of gulls wove the backdrop of sound before which each snippet of speech performed. "You know, he's my man," I heard as I walked down the tier. "You spin the wheel, you get the deal," one philosopher uttered. "Do you know what I'm sayin'?"

"*All right*, you're here with those papers!" Coties exclaimed as I stopped at his cell.

Coties took the newspapers I offered, then pulled out a poem he wanted to include in our anthology. The mother of his children had asked for a love poem, and this was Coties's reply. Coties had told me of the division his imprisonment placed between them, and how they both kept trying to reach across the distance. "Loving and Tender is the sweep of your pen," was the poem's gorgeous first line.

"Glenn," I whispered at the bars of another cell after I'd left Coties and walked downstairs.

Glenn woke slowly, looked toward the bars, and smiled. "It's been a long time since I was woken up by the sound of a woman's voice," Glenn told me.

Glenn kept repeating that he wasn't a poet, though when he showed me something he wrote, I always responded to its sad, lonely longing. On that November afternoon, Glenn shrugged a shy permission, allowing me to use "For Each Day" in our anthology; the poem was inspired by Langston Hughes's "Mother to Son."

I made my way through West Block, stopping to see two other men who had joined our class in the weeks just before this lockdown. Ralph was a large white man who went by the prison moniker of Santa Claus. He was the only one of my students older than I was, and whereas most of the men had been serving time since their early twenties, Ralph had entered prison in his midforties. His poems were rarely about life on the inside; they were most often about his roots in the Midwest in the '30s and '40s.

Smokey was young and striking. Even today, when I show a video of my San Quentin students saying their poems, high school girls swoon over Smokey's black skin and his sexy light eyes. Smokey considered himself more a visual artist than a poet, and over the years, the men in our class would frequently call on him for illustrations to accompany their poems.

I'd saved Spoon for my last stop. As time went on, I felt closer and closer to Spoon. In those weeks before the lockdown, Spoon would leave the spiral staircase when he saw me enter the Plaza each morning and join me as I walked toward Operations. Inside the Arts-in-Corrections office, Spoon would show me a poem he had written or let me tell him about a book I was reading or some thought circling my mind.

Spoon called me his "Big Sis," and though my short, white, round self next to his tall, dark leanness hardly indicated a family photo, this naming felt true. I thought of Spoon as the brother of my soul, a brother who not only shared my shyness and this-and-also-that vision (as Spoon would soon put it: "We all have one foot in light and one foot in darkness"), but one who wanted from me exactly what I could give: my love of poems and my curiosity about consciousness.

Spoon seemed to already know what it had taken that endless wet winter to teach me—that the tone of nature is grief, and entered into, such grief is also a gift. As Spoon continued to write, his poems were suffused with this tone, which, more than their imagery or music, would soon lead others to call Spoon "the Poet."

The shift was changing as I prepared to leave West Block: Second-watch officers were on their way home; third-watch staff was just coming on. The officer who unlocked the gate to release me summed up the slap-on-the-back-of-your-buddy air that just then filled the block's entrance. "You know," he said as he placed the key in the lock, "this job wouldn't be bad if it wasn't for inmates."

....

When people learn I worked for four years at a maximum security prison—spending hundreds of hours in cell blocks with men convicted of capital crimes—the question they most often ask is "Were you afraid?" Each issue of the *San Quentin News* certainly documented one assault or another—inmate against inmate, inmate against guard, guard against inmate. And work at my desk in the Arts-in-Corrections office was quite often punctuated by the sound of alarm whistles going off and the sight of officers running from all over the prison to the site of some trouble. At such times I did frequently wonder how vegetarian, poet, don't-kill-a-fly I had landed here. But this question arose not from terror or dread, but from deepest curiosity.

The truth is, though I experienced a full range of human feelings during my years at the prison, never once did fear triple my heartbeat or soak my sides in cold sweat. Never once did I imagine weapons in students' hands or being backed into some deserted hallway. So, although for most folks, "prison" and "fear" arise as one thought, my honest answer to the question "Were you afraid?" is "No." But, I continue, I did feel many emotions akin to fear. I often wondered with nervous concern whether I—middle-aged, middle-class, academically trained, white, Jewish good girl—had anything to say that would be remotely useful to the men at San Quentin. I would fret at the fact of my shy stuttering self in this world of quick street wit. Nearly everyone at San Quentin was a master of the brilliant retort, while I'd stand and stammer, lost in my head. I often took words so literally, I didn't even know when I was being teased. Once, when I was five, I was eating lunch with my cousin Beryl. I was a very picky eater, and Beryl was encouraging me to finish my food. As she met no success, her voice grew solemn, and she made horse-galloping noises with her feet on the floor. "If you don't eat," Beryl warned, "the sheriff will get you!" I was five, not a baby, and I could see Beryl's thighs rise and lower next to me on the bench where we sat. Still, I believed her: Why in the world would Beryl lie to me? Thirty-four years later at San Quentin, I frequently had to pause after hearing some similarly outrageous statement before I realized, oh, right, he's joking.

Often I brooded over some moment in class—as I had after Elmo pinned me that night I'd asked students to write in response to Hikmet's advice. I could spend days examining my behavior. This self-conscious questioning wasn't a product of prison, though, but simply my nature.

Many times the realities of life for those locked in cells brought me back to my own experiences with despair. My lack of clarity about "boundaries" often left me feeling flooded by the suffering of others. Gabriel's attention caused me discomfort, but what I felt was uneasy, never afraid.

Occasionally I felt a generalized anxiety in class. Sometimes there were undercurrents I didn't understand, but I did sense. Peter, who'd begun teaching drawing on main line, said that Arts-in-Corrections classes were like Switzerland: the one place in prison that was neutral. Men of all races and backgrounds came together with the shared intention of making art. Peter's *bon mot* not only was clever; it contained some truth. Still, differences and outright hostilities among men did not disappear; they were merely put on hold.

Over the years I heard folks in Arts-in-Corrections say, "If something came down, my students would protect me." There was one story—truth or myth, I never found out—of a woman artist on her first night of teaching. The electricity went out, and she was certainly afraid, surrounded as she was by men she did not yet know who might well be serving time for murder or rape. But when the lights again shone, she saw the backs of her students in a circle around her; the men faced outward, prepared to defend her.

I knew my students cared about me. I completely trusted that they would never harm me and would do all they could to make sure no one else did. I knew many of the men in my class were well respected by other prisoners and, therefore, that their wishes had the power to influence behavior. Still, since Elmo's post-Hikmet questions, I tried never to assume what I could not know. So I did not allow myself to believe that my students would be able, in every situation, to provide safety for me.

What I *did* know was that I could count on my students to tell me when they were angry or upset. This meant I didn't have to worry about what was unsaid. Fear arose for me in situations in which there was a discrepancy between what was overtly acknowledged and what my senses picked up. In prison, violence was a given: There were men here who had murdered; there were men here ready to shoot. Having horror out in the open was something like a relief to vibe-conscious me.

Being hyper-alert to what lay beneath the surface, I was used to trusting my own intuition. For example, I walked alone at night and took public transportation at all hours. My attitude was not one of tempting fate, but of resisting a life in which media-created fear controlled all my actions. I preferred to strengthen my ability to sense actual, not theoretical, danger. Over the years at San Quentin, I would notice that relying on bureaucracy's rules, or accepting disparaging generalizations about prisoners, dulled one's human instinct to assess for oneself what was safe and what was not.

The single time I experienced something like fear at San Quentin was the one time I listened to rumor. I'd come to work and found the prison locked down. In Operations, folks were saying staff was going to be hit and that this hit would not be directed at a particular person, but would be random. I went to the blocks to see my students before anyone told me I couldn't, but I was surprised to notice myself walking especially close to the edge of the tier, away from each cell. I realized I was afraid, and not because of what my own body sensed, but because of gossip. This rumor-induced fear fit blinders over my eyes, rendering me incapable of noticing accurately what happened around me, thus putting me at greater risk of real danger.

As hearsay had warned, the lockdown went on for weeks. In mid-December, Stephen Mitchell gave me inscribed copies of his translation of Rilke's *Letters to a Young Poet* for my students. Just before Christmas, I delivered these books. Rilke had written about solitude and bearing sadness, and Mitchell hoped the poet's words might be of use to the men at San Quentin. These men, most of whom were facing the possibility of spending their whole lives in prison, had done their own serious thinking about solitude and sadness.

Rilke had written:

For if we imagine this being of the individual as a larger or smaller room, it is obvious that most people come to know only one corner of their room, one spot near the window, one narrow strip on which they keep walking back and forth. In this way they have a certain security. And yet how much more human is the dangerous insecurity that drives those prisoners in Poe's stories to feel out the shapes of their horrible dungeons and not be strangers to the unspeakable terror of their cells.

My own life had forced me to cover more space than that "one narrow strip" Rilke wrote of. My students' lives had forced the same onto them. Elmo once wrote of feeling out terror in most concrete terms: "A cell measures from the point of my elbow on one arm to the tip of my outstretched fingers on the other. I've measured it a thousand different times, in a hundred different cells, during my years at Q."

The ways my students and I all had felt "out the shapes of [our] horrible dungeons," the ways we each were not "strangers to the unspeakable terrors," as well as the ways in which we all longed for freedom and light, bound us together. So, the main reason I wasn't afraid during my years at San Quentin was that, for me, that quip—"This job wouldn't be so bad if it wasn't for inmates"—was all wrong: "Inmates," the men who were my students, was the precise reason I was here.

five

"Like a Poet"

"Hot dog!" Jim exclaimed as he hung up the receiver, picked up the cloth beanbags always on his desk, and began juggling. The call was from Jan Jonson, Jim announced, a theater director in Sweden.

Jan told Jim that he'd just completed work on a production of Samuel Beckett's *Waiting for Godot* with maximum security prisoners at Sweden's Kumla Prison. Jim and his family had visited Sweden the previous summer; Jim had even been to Kumla and met its warden, Lenart Wilson.

Beckett had heard of Jan's Kumla production and wrote letting Jan know that such work was exactly what he wished for *Godot*. The playwright wanted more details about the project and eventually asked Jan to come meet with him in Paris.

At that meeting, Jan discussed his observation that from its first line—"Nothing to be done"—*Godot* echoed prisoners' lives with their endless waiting for what may never come. Jan talked to Beckett about his desire for a theater created not by actors, but out of the forces and truths of real people's lives. Jan felt that maximum security prisoners playing *Godot* was such theater.

Beckett agreed and mentioned the play's historic connection with San Quentin. The first West Coast production of *Godot* was given by the San Francisco Actors' Workshop. This group performed the play in San Francisco, of course, but also at San Quentin in November 1957. As the drama critic Martin Esslin wrote of this performance, "what had bewildered the sophisticated audiences of Paris, London, and New York was immediately grasped by an audience of convicts." "Godot at San Quentin" became a major chapter in Esslin's classic, *The Theatre of the Absurd*.

The *San Quentin News* wrote at the time:

> It was an expression, symbolic in order to avoid all personal error, by an author who expected each member of his audience to draw his own conclusions, making his own errors. It asked nothing in point, it forced no dramatized moral on the viewer, it held out no specific hope. . . . We're still waiting for Godot, and shall continue to wait. When the scenery gets too drab and the action too slow, we'll call each other names and swear to part forever— but then, there's no place to go!

One inmate who watched that 1957 production was so moved by the play, he went on to form a prison drama workshop. Rick Cluchey gained a pardon and established the San Quentin Players on the outside. He also became a lifelong friend of Beckett's.

Jan wanted to continue working with *Godot* in prison; Beckett was interested in the play's San Quentin connection; Lenart Wilson had recently met Jim. These three facts informed the phone call Jim had just received and resulted in plans for Jan to visit San Quentin in February.

Jim went to see our warden, for gaining his approval was the necessary first step to any potential production. After getting the go-ahead, Jim spent January recruiting prisoners to read for parts in the play. Gabriel was interested, and we'd talked Spoon into at least showing up. Ralph, the new student the others dubbed "Santa Claus," loved *Godot,* saw himself as Estragon, and signed up his friend Mike to read for Vladimir. James also said he'd be there.

James was another man new to my class, but not new to the rest of my students. James was famous. He had been out at court my whole first year at San Quentin, appealing his case. And he'd won. He returned to San Quentin no longer a lifer, but instead with less than two years left to serve. James was a San Quentin hero.

Before I met James, I had seen him. In 1985, the visual artist Jonathan Borofsky and the video artist Gary Glassman made *Prisoners,* a video about prison life. The two artists interviewed thirty-two prisoners at three California prisons. James was one of those interviewed at San Quentin.

I'd watched the video quite a few times; now I saw James in person. James didn't swagger. Maybe his victory in court protected him from the need to swagger, or maybe his age helped. James was in his midthirties, while most men at San Quentin appeared to be close to a decade younger.

Gary Glassman had been so compelled by prison during the making of *Prisoners* with Borofsky that he applied for, and received, his own California Arts Council residency grant at the California Institution for Men near Los Angeles. One of Jim's January tasks was to call Gary and arrange for him to come to San Quentin to videotape the *Godot* readings. Jan would then take these tapes to Beckett, enabling the two men to decide if, from their point of view, a San Quentin production of the play should occur.

For two February evenings Gabriel, Spoon, Ralph, Mike, James, Jim, and I sat in the studio of SQTV, just down the hall from our classroom, listening to Jan's stories. Everyone's favorite was the one in which Jan and his Kumla cast received permission to take *Godot* on the road. The prisoners were free for a few hours to walk around Gothenburg. But when the clock showed barely an hour until curtain and only one of the five men had arrived at the theater, everyone began to worry.

An excited audience had filled the Gothenburg theater. They waited five minutes past opening time; then ten minutes; then fifteen. Jan walked through the curtains at that point and straight to center stage, where he talked about the play and its history at Kumla. Finally, even Jan—raconteur extraordinaire—had to stop telling stories and admit the bald fact: Four-fifths of his cast had escaped!

Every time Jan told the story, he acted the part of a deaf old man in the audience not understanding the uproar around him. This portrayal sent Gabriel into great guffaws. Jan cupped his hand around his ear and squeaked, "What? Has something happened? What did he say?"

Gary presented his own credentials, showing us videos from his class at CIM. Gary told us, "I walked into my class one day and asked, 'Why do these guys whistle at me when I walk past the weight pit?' The men cracked up. They said, 'It's because of the way you *walk*, man. You gotta walk smooth.'" Gary showed us the videotaped lesson his students had prepared on such strutting.

My friend the poet Kate Doughtery was in the middle of her own first year of a CAC grant. She was teaching poetry to the children of Point Arena Elementary School. Sara had graduated from PA Elementary, and over the years we lived in Mendocino county, I had volunteered or been hired to share poetry with almost every child in the school. Kate invited me to come back as a guest artist in the sixth- and eighth-grade classrooms. So after Jan returned to Sweden, I went up coast, I went back home.

Point Arena is close to the westernmost edge of the continental United States; six months of rain are followed by months of high winds, then summer's dense fog. The population of the area around town is four hundred—less than the number of men housed in San Quentin's smallest cell block.

Kate asked me to talk to the sixth graders about picture poems, share Kenneth Patchen's work and Blake's, and bring in reproductions of medieval manuscripts, with their elaborate initials and borders. We thought, though, that I would talk to the eighth graders about San Quentin and read my students' work to them.

We had great fun with the sixth graders, playing with language and image. When these children discovered I'd be reading poems by men in prison to the eighth graders, they asked to be included. Jim Wesley pushed tables and chairs around in his science classroom, and a few dozen eleven-to-fourteen-year-olds filled the room.

Over the years, I have shared prisoner work in a wide variety of school settings. But my visit to Point Arena was the first such encounter, and I didn't know what to expect. Before I read the poems, I described the five tiers of a cell block, the wire mesh over bars, how a man in lockup might exercise outside three or four times each week, but would spend most of his days and nights in a cell.

These were country kids listening, kids who lived surrounded by fields and forests, who fished in the Garcia and Gualala, who surfed in the sea. For all the redwood and fir, for all the fawns and lambs on the hillsides, though, these were kids who spent the bulk of their own days inside a school. These were kids on the brink of adolescence, kids who'd seen their share of TV cops and robbers. They listened intently to the words of the men from San Quentin. They listened to Spoon—a country boy, too, though from the desert, rather than the coast—speak in "Heart of the High Desert," that poem he'd written from my transcription of the words he'd spoken during our first conference:

A wildflower takes its
first breath of air
after a generous rainfall.

They listened to Spoon describe being kept in a cell at the city jail across the street from the high school he had attended, and what he heard from that cell:

the sounds of the games
the football games I'd gone to
my whole life in that town.

They listened to Spoon tell them:

My nephew wrote me a letter
first time in the ten years I've been here.
He wrote he remembers
I taught him to drive,
to whistle.
He remembers washing my car
He wrote, "Dear Uncle Stanley."

The Point Arena kids listened to Glenn as he waited for the officer distributing mail to come by:

As he passes
my tiny cell
I know once again
I have been forgotten.

They listened to the last words of Coties's response to his girlfriend's request for a love poem, that poem he'd shown me three months before in West Block:

Baby, this is my love poem for you.
We're both trying to see through the darkness
you on the outside
me on the inside.

They listened and asked questions, and they told me stories. One girl knew a woman who had been a sergeant at San Quentin; another girl's grandfather had been a cook there. One or two kids had a relative in prison or jail.

86

The kids wanted to know: What jobs did the men do in prison? Did they have children? What were their crimes? Was I ever scared? Finally, a sixth grader, Noah Berlow, burst out, "Let's write them some letters!" The next day their teacher, Nancy Wagner, handed me quite a stack.

Because these kids had been listening to the prisoners' feelings shaped in poem lines, because they themselves had been writing with Kate for almost six months, mostly they wrote poems of their own. And, fresh from our lesson on the combination of words and image, many of these poems were accompanied by an illustration or set off with a fancy initial or border.

The kids wrote poems with lines like these:

Life is a cage
It scares me just thinking
about it.
      —J.J.

and:

within a block
like ice.
      —Autumn

and:

I can see light
and happiness
unlike you.
      —Hollie

and, from a girl who described herself as "a real crazy kid":

Even though I have seen
all of it on television

it didn't even cross my
mind after 10 minutes
from watching a movie
that there is a real
person in prison.
When I heard the poems
and the writing of the
prisoners, I
took a piece of their
sorrow . . .
　　　　—Jibs

And that Thursday in February, during a furious Point Arena rainstorm, they wondered more deeply about the men's lives:

What Is It Like?
It was a cold
winter day
when the rain
was pouring down
and the wind
was blowing hard and fast.
The trees were breaking.
What is it like there?
Does it have floods
rainstorms? What
is it like?
　　　　—Matthew

and about their pain:

You are like a
baby bird trapped in an
egg   it is dark   no freedom
no friend you can't get out
inside   you crying

88

but you can't show it
you have to be a
man
you have to be
strong   if you are
not strong you
will not survive.
          —Danny

These kids wondered what it would be like to make a mistake so big it would change your whole life:

The memories
of a prisoner
are hard to take
Your loneliness
and grief
You think of the moon
the stars and
the world around you
You think of your
loved ones
and your
unhappy life
you go back
and want to
start your
life over again.
          —Laney

It was to Spoon, especially, the kids addressed their letters and poems. Spoon—whose world included wildflowers and butter-flies, as did their world. Spoon—a country kid who "was nineteen when I got busted." Spoon—who would write in a poem later that year:

Over two years ago
I knew nothing of
poetry
Of how it allows a
huge part of me to
be free.
How the truth in
it makes people feel
how it allows me
to feel love and sorrow
like a great earthquake
starting from
so deep
within

I cradled the bundle of children's poems and hurried into town to call Jim. I'm sure the river of words I poured through the phone lines flooded out all actual detail, but Jim caught my obvious joy.

"Well, you'll show me on Monday," Jim said with excitement enough to sustain me.

I stood in the phone booth, trying to avoid getting soaked in the storm, and looked across the street at Gilmore's. I remembered how three years earlier I'd stood outside that all-purpose store pinning a deckle-edged pink sheet of paper to the bulletin board. I had just printed a small poem on the thick paper, and I wanted to share Wendell Berry's words with whoever paused to read them. The wind that had torn through town all that day had died down, and as I stood outside Gilmore's that long ago March evening, I'd laughed: thirty-seven years old and still wanting to be the Lone Ranger, riding into town in the dark night, leaving gifts.

Now, however, back in this phone booth during a February storm, I knew I no longer wanted to hide behind some Lone Ranger mask. Those post-Hikmet questions Elmo had asked me—Who was I? Why was I here?—were the questions I'd lived my life asking. When I was younger, I'd assumed I was supposed to come up with an answer. But the voice I had let myself trust on leaving my marriage told me instead to give up such willful pretense, and to live an unmasked life of surrender.

Just before this trip to Point Arena, I'd been to lockup teaching cell to cell. That day I'd taken a Rilke poem about being shaped by submission to share with the men. I stood on the tier reading the poem to Dennis:

> *What we choose to fight is so tiny!*
> *What fights with us is so great!*
> *If only we would let ourselves be dominated*
> *as things do by some immense storm*
> *we would become strong too, and not need names.*
> *When we win it's with small things,*
> *and the triumph itself makes us small.*
> *What is extraordinary and eternal*
> *does not want to be bent by us. . . .*

I continued to the poem's last lines:

> *This is how he grows: by being defeated, decisively,*
> *by constantly greater beings.*

I slipped the sheet through the slight space to the far left of Dennis's cell, through a tiny gap between mesh-over-bars and the concrete wall that separated his cell from the next.

Dennis looked over the poem. He hesitated in a way I took to mean he was glad for my weekly presence and support of his writing: He didn't want to offend me. But the need to speak his truth won out.

"It's a tight poem," Dennis acknowledged, "but I hate what he says. He wants god; I'm more into the devil."

The enthusiastic fast pace I relied on to get me through the pain of being in lockup slammed into the wall of Dennis's words.

"The devil?"

"Yes."

"What's the devil?" I asked.

"What's the devil?" Dennis repeated. "*I'm* the devil. I wake up in the morning and ask what is it *I* want, what do *I* want to do? Then I do it."

I'd been astonished by Dennis's precise definition and found I agreed, such selfish will *was* the devil. And I agreed, too, with Dennis's implied corollary that surrender was the devil's opposite. Where I disagreed was with Dennis's view that such letting go was weak. As I walked out of the block, I remembered the moment I first recognized submission as courage.

It had been during that long journey through Europe after leaving my marriage. One day I hitchhiked the short distance from the English Lake District to the small town of Hawes in the Yorkshire Dales. It was raining, as usual, and the hostel wouldn't open for another few hours. I walked for a while, getting thoroughly soaked, and then climbed the stairs to the town's open-three-afternoons-a-week library. When the librarian, a woman about my own age, saw me, she immediately asked for my jacket and shoes and she set these by the heater to dry. I sat down by this heater, with a volume of Wordsworth I'd taken from the poetry shelf. When the day's few patrons had selected their books and departed, the librarian made us both tea and asked for my story.

She shook her head and spoke of my courage. She herself had been born in Hawes and still lived just down the road with her husband and children. She liked her life fine, but often thought of traveling, of setting out on her own. She couldn't believe I had really done what she'd let herself only dream of.

Many times on this journey, people mentioned my courage. Courage? I didn't see it. Courage seemed what was required of heroes of old. I wasn't following dreams, and I wasn't courageous; I simply felt I had no other choice. But as the afternoon wound down, and the librarian from Hawes talked of her longings, I saw that maybe that's all courage is: Doing as best as you're able what life asks you to do.

In that Point Arena phone booth, after I'd called Jim, I realized that we all choose the way we'll tell our own stories. Others might look at my life through the lens of psychological illness, white middle-class privilege, coming-of-age-in-the-'60s insistence on discarding old structures, self-centered indulgence, or—as the folks at San Quentin saw me—the ways of a "free spirit." Any of these descriptions could frame the events and emotions I'd lived through.

But I chose to see my life as a spiritual journey. That voice I listened to sounded to me like unfolding existence, and my surrender as aligning myself with what inevitably is.

When Sara and I decided to move from Point Arena back to the city, there was a lot that I wanted: I wanted more varied teaching, I wanted more opportunities to attend poetry readings and to give them myself, I wanted to walk down streets surrounded by a variety of faces and tongues, I wanted a less inbred life than Point Arena High would give Sara. So maybe Dennis would see our move as my vote for the devil and will.

But I saw leaving Point Arena as upping the ante, as asking those *Who am I? Why am I here?* questions harder. Who would I be amidst noise and pollution, working many more hours to pay rent on a small apartment? Asking these questions had brought me to San Quentin. And that February Thursday, one day before my fortieth birthday, San Quentin seemed exactly where I needed to be.

When I walked into the prison Monday morning, there was Spoon across the Plaza, sitting in that spiral staircase. As he did most mornings, Spoon joined me as I walked to the Arts-in-Corrections office.

On this particular morning, I was so excited by what had happened in Point Arena, I hardly took time to say hello. I knew how much these poems would mean to all my students, but I knew they would mean most to Spoon. I told him how the kids had listened to the men's poems and that they decided, on their own, to write to the poets. I told him how much the kids had loved his poems in particular. Then I pulled out the stack of papers I'd brought from Point Arena.

Two years later, Spoon would write of this moment: "I hardly ever smiled or took my shades off, even on the most wonderful of days—I'd keep the wonder inside me. But, as I began to read the poems and letters, I was unable to contain the magnificence, the sheer magic, and realness jumping off the pages into my heart and soul."

I showed Spoon the kids' words, but didn't give them to him: I had to get permission first. So, as Spoon went off to his prison job, I waited for Jim.

Jim was as excited as I was as he pored over the kids' poems, drawings, and ornate initials. He, too, was touched by the care, craft, and compassion of these youngsters. He, too, could see how well the children had caught not only the feelings but the tone of the men's poems. (Laney had written in her note to Spoon: "This poem is almost like your poems.") I talked of a prisoner-student poem exchange, and Jim expanded on the idea: Maybe we could videotape the guys reading their poems and send this tape around to schools. He picked up on the words of one child: "If you ever get out of that jail place, I hope you guys will try writing more po-etry. Hearing an experienced prisoner tell all about the place, peo-ple would want to hear so they won't wind up in jail."

What better way, Jim thought out loud, to let the kids see what prison is really like? Not the blood and guts glory of TV movies, but loneliness and regret and claiming one's dignity in an envi-ronment designed to deny it.

Although we went off into a chain of "we could do this, we could do that" fantasies, we still knew we were in San Quentin, a maxi-mum security prison run on a strict system of rules. And one primary prison rule prohibits carrying any material from the outside into the institution for an inmate. These poems didn't seem to be the kind of "material" referred to, but Jim certainly wouldn't give the poems to Spoon without consulting with his supervisor.

However, Luis wasn't in his office, and we didn't know when he would arrive. As the morning progressed, Jim and I kept getting ourselves more and more worked up over the power of art and the power of honest human sharing, so that finally, Jim decided I should go ahead and give copies of the poems to Spoon. "If that's a mistake," Jim said in prison parlance, "I'll take the heat."

When Luis did arrive after his day of meetings, Jim let me rush into his office. Luis also responded to the openness of the kids' poems, but after listening to me read—after giving me free rein to ooh and aah my pleasure—he said, "I'm not sure we can give these to Spoon."

I knew Luis approved of the work Jim and all of Arts-in-Corrections was doing, so I didn't restrain myself. I questioned, held forth. Luis didn't interrupt me, but when I stopped, he asked, "What if one of the inmates in your class gets out, goes to that school, and harms one of these kids?"

Kate and I had been very careful: No addresses were given, only first names were used, and we devised a system of parental permission with Nancy Wagner for any correspondence that might take place in the future. Still, the possibility Luis described had never really entered my mind.

"Besides," Luis added, "we don't want to be setting up inmates as some kind of positive role model."

This got me going again. For although it was true that there was one girl who wrote, "It would be really neat to have a pen pal who was in prison. I would like to tell my friends what it's like and show them my letters you sent me," and a few instances of identification with the downtrodden—"I am a fourteen-year-old convict from Point Arena Elementary Penitentiary"—such comments were few and far between.

The shared theme of the children's response was: "I loved the poems. They were great. They made me think, 'Wow, there's real people in there!'" And this realization made the kids wonder about the lived lives of these men: "I used to go fishing by your prison. I could hear you guys do your exercises." Apparently the kids were capable of making distinctions, of recognizing the human beings who had written the poems and, at the same time, of realizing that many of these men had done serious harm to other people. The kids wrote:

> *Their eyes are soft and gentle*
> *But I wonder what*
> *they did*
> *to deserve this place.*

They pondered:

> After being there for a while, you must have thought about what you've done and wished you could start life all over again. The prison probably doesn't treat you well and there isn't much to do, but I bet the worst punishment of all is loneliness.

and:

> In a way, it's really sad that some of the guys have a family at home and their wives need them. But I guess if they would not have committed the crime, they would be at home, living happily ever after.

The next day, Luis told us we'd have to get the poems back from Spoon. The official decision was that I could make photocopies available for the men in my class to read, but neither Spoon nor any other class poet could keep these papers, and there absolutely could not be any exchange of letters.

I had a special class set up for that afternoon, and Spoon was one of the men on the movement sheet. Jim, willing as usual to bear the brunt of the burden, spoke to Spoon on his way to class. When Spoon joined Coties, Glenn, and me, his sunglasses were back on, his face again a fixed surface he lived behind.

At home that night I cried as I told Sara what had happened; I cried on the phone telling Kate. But Kate wasn't crying; she was confused and angry. What was this censorship, and what had happened to me that I so easily submitted to it?

Censorship. In my heart, of course, I felt these poems—prisoner poems read to children, kids' poems written to prisoner poets— honored what was most compassionate and human in both the children and the men. In my heart, I felt a further exchange could only be for the good—for the good of Spoon Jackson and Noah Berlow, and for the good of the spirit that lives within every human being, needing only to be nourished and nurtured.

But already, my time at San Quentin had taught me that my heart, though wholly right in its sight, saw only part of the picture. Already, my time had taught me to remember that some men whom I knew as kind and caring had also caused great harm to other people. Already, my time had taught me I didn't know everything.

In the unambiguous world of my heart's sight, I could always respond with moral assurance. In the more ambiguous world of San Quentin, there was always another point of view. In the ambiguous world of San Quentin, I believed in my heart's sight and, simultaneously, was forced to acknowledge all I didn't know. In the ambiguous world of San Quentin, I received dozens of lessons weekly from Paradox, the great teacher whose spirit I'd actually summoned with all those quotes on my wall.

My tears that night were for Spoon and the kids, who met each other with such open hearts, minds, and souls, and who spoke so clearly through poetry. So this is how the questions that had moved me from Point Arena were being answered? I couldn't believe that less than one week before I'd stood across the street from Gilmore's, full of gratitude for all San Quentin was giving me.

Well, I felt no gratitude now. Instead I wanted to tear all those quotes off my wall. I wanted an unambiguous, unparadoxical world in which openness of heart, mind, and soul were enough, would by themselves cure every ill, every harm done.

Still, I knew my tears, though real, were easy. I could go home, cry on Sara's shoulder, talk with Kate, take a long walk. Spoon had only his cell, its barred gate facing the gun rail.

Of course, Spoon had something else I had let myself forget, although I was the one who had talked and talked of its value.

When I entered the prison the next day, Spoon was not on the spiral staircase, but he appeared at the office shortly after I opened the door. He said nothing, but handed me a typed piece of paper. A poem.

Right Now I Choose Sadness
to the students at Point Arena Elementary School
who sent me their poems and letters

She wrote me today
and asked me
Is everyone there
on death row?
At first I said no
then I began to wonder
could it be so?

I had hoped to write you all back
to share with you
and to thank you all
Your poems and letters are so real
and full of life
and greeted me with tremendous beauty.

The whole day was enhanced with such joy
I walked around smiling inside and out
I truly felt like a poet.

Thank you for taking me beyond
the walls of San Quentin.

Today your poems and letters
were taken from my hands
Still your letters and poems
lie solid within my spirit and heart.

At least I got to see them
people say
Words sometimes do not fill the space
just like one drop of water
does not make an ocean
nor a river.

As I sit in this dark cage
sad music and silence to assuage
this deep wound
in my heart
and spirit
I think of your poems and letters
and how naturally they went to my heart . . .
no detours.

Right now I choose sadness
over happiness
for I feel like a river that has been dammed
or drained.

six

"In the Very Essence of Poetry There Is Something Indecent"

I showed "Right Now I Choose Sadness" to Luis, who liked it so much, he requested a copy. "Ironic," Spoon said when I asked for his permission to give Luis the poem. "Paradoxical." Handing Spoon's poem to Luis was paradoxical, all right, and I marveled again that I'd actually desired such paradox.

San Quentin's schooling was harsher than I'd reckoned upon. But once I stopped crying, I realized I still appreciated the prison's daily challenge that I notice my own assumptions and then move beyond them.

For I had certainly walked into San Quentin in August 1985 with assumptions. My automatic sympathies went to the powerless who, in this situation, I perceived to be the men behind bars. I was still singing "Which Side Are You On?" and still replying, "on the side of those without power."

The first year of once-a-week teaching intensified my innate reaction. For in those months, except for the information and advice given by Jim, what I knew about San Quentin was held within the three solid walls, and the one wall of half-glass, that shaped our buried classroom: What I knew about this foreign world I had entered came from my students. I very much liked each one of the men who made up our core group—Angel, Coties, Elmo, Gabriel, Glenn, Richard, and Spoon—in alphabetical order. And, besides, they were my *students*. Support for the underdog, friendly feelings, and honoring what I felt to be the holiness of the student-teacher relationship conspired to make me a partisan.

In addition, I had walked into San Quentin full of assumptions about guards. During that first year I spent very little time with staff or administration and a great deal of time focused on my students, so my prejudice continued unchecked. This prejudice was born from my natural antiauthoritarianism, from the 1960s rhetoric I'd come of age hearing, and from what I'd seen with my own eyes.

During one antiwar demonstration in Berkeley, for example, I was with a group chased into an underground garage by two policemen. Most of us backed ourselves up against the structure's concrete walls, but one man climbed onto a car and attempted escape through a high window. A policeman grabbed him, dragged him down from the car, and repeatedly beat him. When I thought of "police," when I thought of "prison guard," when I thought of "criminal justice," it was that cop's nightstick raised for a blow that I saw; it was the whack of the baton on the protester's body that I heard.

The dehumanizing sentiments I heard staff express when I first entered the prison—all those "bozo/yo-yo/asshole" characterizations—reinforced my prejudices. Instances where I observed one guard or another flaunt some petty power confirmed my beliefs.

But, now, working under the grant took me beyond the walls of our classroom, into cell blocks and offices. In these situations, I experienced moments that ran counter to the anticop assumptions I carried. At such moments, I had to acknowledge that those representing the badge were, in addition to being agents of authority, also individual human beings with a wide range of personal traits.

Moment: When Phavia had visited the previous year, Luis spoke like a poet: "Gemini," he said of his sons. "The sign of split birth."

"Mexicans always have boys," Luis intoned.

That same evening Luis told Phavia and me about his college days in the Chicano movement. He asked if we'd read Corky Gonzales, a Chicano hero-poet from that era. "A revolutionary," Luis said. "Poets are *always* revolutionaries." Luis delivered this judgment not as a warning, but nearly as praise.

Moment: I'd walked into Luis's office to have him sign some proposal for our class, then sat there and listened. "I'm in a position of authority over people who grew up the same way I did," Luis said. "Mostly, your blue-collar criminal is watched by your blue-collar worker. One time there was a problem with Mexicans on the yard, and I called down to the officers, 'What are you guys doin' to my people?' The sergeant called back, 'Those aren't your people.' But, you know? He wasn't even close."

Moment: One afternoon I walked through Education with Officer DeSantis. We passed a desk and DeSantis picked up a drawing I would have passed right by. Staff, like convicts, tended to be alert to the periphery for anything might be a sign of trouble.

"Hey, look at this," Officer DeSantis said.

He pointed to the pentacle at the center of the page. "That's a sign of the devil. And these," his fingers brushed the shapes that fanned from the five-pointed star, "these are demons. There's no way to erase these," DeSantis continued. "You can only burn the paper itself."

I listened, confused.

"I read about Satanism and try to imagine why anyone would spend so much time drawing an image of the devil. There's only one answer: He must be possessed."

I guess I looked stunned, for DeSantis raised his hand. "Listen, don't get me wrong; I'm no Bible-belter. But to me, an image is real. I'm part Indian, must be from that. I believe in the power of image."

I started to say, "Well, I'm an artist, and I believe in the power of image myself," but prisoners were now walking into the building for afternoon outcount, DeSantis got busy taking their IDs, and we had no time for further discussion.

Moment: Every day Felix, the second-watch officer at Scope Gate, handed out candy, bought with his own money, to everyone passing through the checkpoint during his eight-hour shift. Candy and kind words to staff; candy and kind words to family and friends coming in to visit prisoners.

Moment: One night, while I was teaching a class at the medium security H-Unit outside the prison's walls, the lieutenant on duty stopped by. The men and I all looked up, expecting some kind of problem. Instead, the lieutenant launched into a by-heart rendition of "The Cremation of Sam McGee," his favorite poem.

Moment: I sat in our office and watched prisoners drop by across the hall to see Associate Warden Tabash. "You don't agree with their crime by treating inmates fairly and equitably," Henry often said. "They were sent here *as* punishment, not to *be* punished."

As I acknowledged that, like any group, the staff was composed of unique individuals, I became more curious about the nuanced ways in which these men and women looked at the world. I wondered who I might be if I found myself in a guard's situation.

My first chance to put myself in something like a guard's shoes came in early February, just before my trip up coast to Point Arena. The filmmaker Les Blank had given Arts-in-Corrections copies of his music and culture videos. We had Lydia Mendoza, Lightning Hopkins, Clifton Chenier, the Balfa Brothers, Flaco Jimenez, and others to show in classes and on SQTV. We arranged a screening schedule with folks at the internal television station, and I made a poster to let prisoners know.

It was easy to get copies of this poster to those on main line, but I was stymied for a while about how to get the word to men in lockup. I decided to ask permission to go into the blocks myself to deliver the schedule to these one thousand men.

Even with my experience on the Row with Lynnelle and my own cell-to-cell teaching—which should have provided ample warning—I entered the units with every intention of looking each man in the face. I assumed we'd exchange a few friendly words, and then I'd slide the poster into his cell. In my enthusiastic go-for-it mode I thought, hey, I have all afternoon. I can smile for four hours, no problem.

I managed such smiles for, maybe, one hour. After that, the usual cell block oppression—the heat, the smells, the noise, the sight of five tiers with their opposing gun rails, the fact that each lonely man was capable of talking to a sympathetic soul for hours, the sheer number of men who told me they couldn't *get* TV reception in their block and asked if I'd do something about it—wore me down. At the end of four hours, I could barely speak or look at the man on the other side of the bars, let alone smile. At the end of four hours, I'd nearly stopped caring.

So, what about guards? I wondered. What about those men and women who spent eight hours each day in these units, taking up meals, delivering mail, escorting men to the showers? Even if an officer had the best heart in the world, how would he or she ever be able to manage being decent eight hours a day, five days a week, under these conditions? Was there a Berkeley revolutionary who could manage that?

....

When I was ten, there was a book in my mother's bookcase that told of a marriage and its dissolution. You first opened the pages to read the husband's story. Then you turned the book over and upside down and the story began anew, told this time by the wife.

Trying to find "truth" in prison was like reading this book about marriage. For example, in the long lockdown we'd just come through, I'd go from the Operations Building, where I'd hear staff talk about shanks being found, about missing metal, and rumors of stabbings, to the cell blocks, where some of the men regarded the lockdown as a way for the administration to prove that prison was a dangerous place so that it could ask the legislature for increased funding.

Elmo, my tour guide, said that prison by its very nature was adversarial: There were two sides, convicts and cops, and a prisoner had to draw lines to protect his basic human dignity. I knew that if I wanted to glimpse the whole these adversaries were each part of—as Bresson had urged me to do—I must first pay attention to each individual position.

I'd always been interested in point of view, as a literary tool and as a detail of consciousness. The first experience of shifting perspective I noted occurred when I was five, standing at the ocean's edge with my father. He wanted me to join him in the water, but I stood on shore, very afraid. He tried to convince me that those waves causing me terror were, in fact, harmless and small. Finally he stopped talking and bent down until his head was level with my own. "Goodness," he said. "Those waves sure are big from down here!"

I was accustomed to lending my eyes to my father's sight, but that August afternoon at the beach he'd brought himself in line with *my* vision. He had acknowledged my perception.

Despite this early gift, I often had trouble holding onto my vision; I spent much of my life assuming that if someone else's point of view made sense, my own must be wrong. In many ways, this self-doubt gave birth to me as a writer. For in writing words down on paper, or making up stories in my head, I could see what I saw without also considering someone else's viewpoint or having to explain myself clearly in my father's language. In my imagination, I was free from interference.

Not that either of my parents intended to interfere. Both of them loved and supported me; each valued language. My mother spent much of her time in an armchair reading a novel; one of her daily joys was completing the newspaper's crossword puzzle. My father made up the bedtime stories he told my sister and me, encouraged us to find words to express our feelings, and loved puns.

(My father often repeated the first poem he had composed when he was a small boy: "There is no peace/in the pen with the geese." Rhymed couplets were his form of choice. Once, when a high school English teacher asked me to bring in a permission note before he'd let me read a Tennessee Williams play, my father wrote a poem that included this couplet: "Why then wait for the mañana/ to read 'The Night of the Iguana'?")

My father certainly had a playful imagination and enjoyed joking with words, but primarily, he believed in meaning, in the literal. When I was three, sleeping alone in the room where one year before my father had told me of my brother's death, white light scanned the sky each night and shone through the window at the side of my bed. I was afraid to lie in the pool of this light. My father called what I saw a "searchlight," and told me it was nothing to fear. I trusted he wasn't lying and could even picture the machine he described a few blocks to the south, where the beam narrowed down to a source. Still, I knew what I knew: This circling light was a pathway, a trail witches rode to their home. I knew those witches wanted me to join them, and I'd lie in their light night after night, eyes open, unable to sleep.

The images and phrases that moved through my head as a child— my reality—didn't lend themselves to the kind of language my father valued. My mind naturally made quick, leaping, poetic connections that could only be explained to my father's satisfaction through a process of what felt to me like reduction. But I loved my father and knew he loved me, knew he had my best interests at heart, so I tried to find words that made sense to him.

In my imagination, though, I was free from this effort of translation. The price of this freedom was hiding behind that Lone Ranger mask: I kept my truth hidden to protect it. However, as I'd realized in that Point Arena phone booth, I now wanted to remove the mask.

During my first weeks at San Quentin, I wrote down the words I heard when listening to officers in Four Post or my students in class. I cherished these found poems: "They don't make dumb convicts, not for a long time;" "Never call your cell home."

I also began to write first-person poems in my own voice, such as the one I'd shared with my students about that moment after class when they entered the dark on their way to the blocks and I walked out of the prison and into a world of "bridge lights and town lights and stop lights and shop lights." "So much light," I wrote, "and still I can't see."

And then, the found poems next to poems from my point of view gave birth to poems in voices neither overheard nor my own. My lifelong tendency to see others' viewpoints more clearly than mine had the upside of allowing me to cross thresholds easily. Now voices of imagined prisoners, imagined guards, and imagined folks on the outside flowed through me. Poems in his voice and her voice and his voice and my voice accumulated to create a long sequence. This sequence made me happy, for I felt I'd been given a form that enabled me to observe through a larger lens and to do as Bresson had asked: "Accustom the public to divining the whole of which they are given only part."

I *was* happy, that's true, but as I wrote, the voice of my old critic, Doubt, hissed in my ear: "You're exploiting your students' lives for your poems!" "You're an outsider; you have nothing relevant to say!" "You're a fraud; you'd better stop writing."

I spoke back to Doubt: "I'm not writing about prison, I'm writing about the whole we're each part of. I can write about that; that's mine; that's how I see the world!" In my argument with Doubt, I imposed two ironclad rules on myself as I wrote: To use nothing personal anyone had actually told me, and never to indulge in irony or distance, but instead to enter completely the world of the imagined speaker so that I spoke fully informed by how he or she saw the world.

When I stated the question bluntly—did those of us teaching in prison have a right to let our own artwork be affected by what we were experiencing?—the answer was simple. To be affected, and then to give witness, was a primary task of the artist. But when Doubt's voice pounded in my ears, I was less sure.

Lynnelle told me about a time she was working in a lockup unit. "Each cell had a window, with bars on the inside, that was kept shut. I would knock on this twelve-by-twelve-inch window, open it, and talk to the guy through it. All I could see was each man's head and these bars. Of course, the bars were about eye width apart, so I never had direct eye contact with the man I was talking to.

"This was such a strong visual image, I wanted to do some drawing. At first these drawings were too literal: a face and the bars. This wasn't really what I wanted to show. Finally I broke through to being able to draw the bars and the face and the man's features with one line, appearing as one form. These were some of the strongest drawings I have ever done."

Lynnelle encouraged me to persist with my poems. She gave me permission to encounter this world we had entered and to let what I wrote be shaped by what touched my senses. Lynnelle and I, and most of those teaching with Arts-in-Corrections, were not famous. But we were people for whom painting or writing poems or playing bass was essential; to create was why we were here on this planet. We had whatever feelings we had about lack of worldly recognition, but recognized or not, being an artist was at the center of each of our beings.

I had read a few of the earliest poems from this series to my class the previous summer, and now I wanted to read more from the work. These poems expressed how I saw the world and I was very excited to share them with my students.

However, the phrase "my students" now indicated a larger group of men. Many prisoners had seen me in West Block during the lockdown, and, when they discovered there was a poetry class, they signed up to attend. Though I'd talked with each of these men individually, we'd hardly met as a group. The officer taking afternoon count on Mondays was new and extremely slow, which resulted in a series of late counts and, consequently, canceled classes. Though prudence would have had me wait and let this new grouping of men coalesce, my desire to share these poems was so strong that on an evening in early March, I just went ahead.

Eleven men sat around the two tables I'd placed together. Elmo, Gabriel, Spoon, James, Ralph, Glenn, and Smokey were there, as were four others—Carl, Chris, a new Leo, and Sammy—who had joined class after the lockdown. Coties was at court.

As soon as the men settled down, I introduced my poems and began reading "Count's cleared and the guard says . . ." Many men had heard this one, but I soon shared poems that were new to them. In one a guard says:

> *I know how I'm thought of*
> *as some kind of Nazi*
> *a man who takes pleasure*
> *in control over others.*
> *You think I'm sadistic*
> *that seeing men locked in cages*
> *or a gun on my hip*
> *gets me off.*
>
> *Well, I tell you you're wrong.*
> *Just try spending eight hours*
> *in one of these blocks.*
> *Five tiers, steel and concrete;*
> *odor the essence of dungeon.*
> *Four gates on each tier*
> *and I tell you the keys*
> *must weigh more than a gun does . . .*

I read a poem in the voice of a woman on the outside, whose young daughter had been raped and then murdered:

> *I still want to tell her*
> *Baby, that's not what sex is.*
> *Sex is good, you'll see.*

Halfway through the reading, Elmo shoved his chair away from the table, rose nosily, and stomped into the hall. I could hear him talking to someone out there as alarm whistles—like those that shrieked loudly over San Quentin's grounds, setting staff running—wailed now all over my body.

When I came to the end of the last poem, Elmo walked back into the classroom and said, "How dare you write about this world that isn't yours?"

Chris had stayed seated during my reading, but he nodded. "Now, you *know* poems like these feed the public's anti-con attitudes. Why would you write poems like that?"

"But . . . " I started to sputter, summoning all my will not to let the catch in my voice expand into the cry now spiraling inside me. Despite my effort, I felt the tears in my eyes spill over my cheeks. I barely knew Chris, so it wasn't his words ripping me open. I felt so close to Elmo, though, and he was clearly upset—not just upset, but upset at me. Was he really so angry because I'd written a poem from the point of view of a decent guard? I wanted to ask, "What about the poems in the voice of prisoners? What about the ones that say:

> I've got life without possibility of parole.
> Life without.
> Life without helping my kids do their homework,
> without taking my mother to church . . .

or:

> . . . who I am. A man
> who once was a boy.
> A man with hands that know
> how to shape, how to be gentle,
> how to touch what they love."

But I didn't trust my voice not to shatter, so I said nothing.

For a long while, everyone else in the room was also quiet. I felt us all doing our best to stay still enough to contain the emotions—anger, hurt, and some others I didn't know quite how to read, though they seemed pointed and ugly—that threatened to overtake us. In that group effort, those metaphoric alarm whistles quieted down sufficiently for some real conversation.

Elmo and Chris wanted to know if I was just another outsider walking into San Quentin inviting them to open up, then using what I saw and heard to exploit them. "Seems to me, you're using our pain for your gain," Elmo said. If Elmo was right, if I was exploiting my students' suffering for my own ends, such an act went beyond betrayal: Such an act was my definition of evil.

Most of the other men continued to be silent. Glenn, who rarely spoke, asked about writing from a point of view not your own. "Could a man really write like he was a woman having a baby?" Glenn asked. "I don't see how he could."

This question allowed me to assume a teacher's voice and talk about the history of literature: There would be no such thing as novels and plays if what Glenn described was not possible. Then Carl asked a question about rhyme, and we were able to spend the rest of the evening talking technique.

Gabriel walked beside me up the stairs after class, but when we reached the top, I walked over to Elmo. He was standing in the corner, alone. As soon as he saw me he said, "I thought I could trust you, that's why I've told you so much. I told you both my parents had died, and you used that line in one of your poems."

"Both my parents have died," yes, I remembered the line, and I remembered Elmo telling me this fact from his life. But I hadn't thought of Elmo's truth when I wrote the poem; I'd just thought of very large loss.

On that Monday night in early March, I didn't know how profoundly Elmo had felt the passing of his parents, and so didn't realize just how much trust he'd placed in me by telling me of their deaths. That Monday night, I didn't fully realize the emotional risk

Elmo had taken by choosing to be open with someone in an environment he would later describe as one in which "truth and trust are rare commodities." But I understood that, though I'd felt attacked, Elmo felt betrayed.

I had been as conscious as I could be and had still managed to break my own rule: use nothing personal anyone had told me. I'd written the best that I was able, and had hurt someone I cared for. For a long string of moments I thought, "Well, I'll just stop writing."

But what I asked Elmo was, "I can't believe we've been working together for eighteen months and now, at my first bad mistake, you're not willing to extend me any grace at all?"

"I'm talking with you, aren't I?" Elmo responded. "If it wasn't for those eighteen months, I'd have walked right out; you'd never have seen me again."

Sara was sleeping when I got home, but her sweet face on her pillow gave me enough courage to encounter the night. I put away all the books and papers I'd carried to the prison, placed the poems I'd just read back in their folder, then sat down in that same bentwood rocking chair I'd rocked in that night long ago when Elmo first asked me hard questions. This ordering calmed me—here's home, here's where I'm safe. I settled myself in the rocker and watched what arose.

I knew my body, in that basement classroom, had reacted as though attacked. Alarm whistles had gone off inside me, and not just for me, but for us all: I'm in danger, this group is in danger.

I saw how, as a group, we had managed the necessary stillness and attention to let tremendous passion be held in that room. Because I didn't know well all the men who composed the new configuration of our class, I wasn't sure how to name the feelings precisely. But I knew emotion burned hot in that room and as I sat in my rocker at midnight, I was very much impressed with our shared ability to contain what might easily have burst into flame.

My own feelings felt hurt. My students had questioned my poems, these poems I'd been so excited to share. I'd read these same poems on the north coast on the night of my fortieth birthday. Some in the audience let me know they were offended by my intensity. I knew what they perceived was true: I was driven. Bresson's "Make people diviners" injunction was delivered in the same steady, straightforward tone as his films were. My nervous system was not nearly so stable, and my jumpiness led me to grab folks by the shoulders and shout: Look, look at this.

Now some of my students seemed to be saying that since I wasn't locked behind bars, I didn't have the right to speak about prison. If I had been able to talk without crying, I would have told the men in my class that in my mind, my poems were less about prison and more about consciousness. To me, my poems were "about" how what each of us sees is all there is to the one who is seeing, but only part of the picture when looked at from a wider angle. To me, the poems were about the knowledge that there *is* a wider angle, even if we can't measure it by degrees.

Still, at least some of my students wanted to make sure I acknowledged that my poems were also about prison. And if I was going to speak of their turf, I'd better tread with utmost care.

Whatever hurt their words had caused me, I knew Elmo and Chris had raised a serious point: Prisoners were vulnerable to each of us who walked in from the outside. I didn't feel my poems exploited my students; I knew that wasn't my intention, and I didn't see exploitation as being the effect of the poems. However, I understood that simply writing about the world my students endured put me in jeopardy of taking advantage of their suffering.

Something deep in me hated relationships of unequal power, and this aversion often made me pretend that my students and I were all equal in an equitable world. Such pretense was harmful, however, both to me and to my students. For the reality was that, although all these men were bigger and stronger—and most of them full of more anger—than I was, I was the one with authority. I was the one likely to be believed in any altercation. I didn't want to accept this fact, but I could see that pretending otherwise was a "false innocence" none of us could afford.

Okay. Danger, hurt, sadness, accusations, and self-deception—all these were fairly easy to face sitting there in my rocking chair fifteen miles from San Quentin, my sweet daughter asleep down the hall, our cat in my lap. But the closer I got to looking at Elmo, specifically Elmo and all he had told me, the faster my heart beat.

Elmo's size, forceful male presence, and articulate speech could certainly be intimidating, but it wasn't these that made me want to crawl under the covers to avoid through sleep what I was feeling. Instead, the pain swirling inside me was twofold. First, Elmo felt I'd betrayed him. Letting this fact come close to my heart nearly ripped me apart. Writing was too dangerous: I could write the best I was able, with as much consciousness as I could muster, and still hurt someone badly. In the world of prison, which Elmo had described to me so many times as a war zone, he had chosen to trust me. He'd chosen, despite all the prison rules that made simple human sharing so risky, to tell me a sacred fact of his life. And, though I hadn't meant to, I'd abused this trust.

The very permeability of mind that allowed poetry, also made poems perilous. When I wrote the poem with that line—"both my parents have died"—I didn't for one moment think of the words Elmo had told me. But he had told me those words, and somehow, somewhere, they must have stayed with me. The poem then called on those words. This unconscious process now scared me.

Months earlier, I'd experienced a somewhat similar shock. I was working on a poem, and I was stuck and—as often happens to me in that state—suddenly sleepy. I lay down for a few minutes and woke up with the line "Comprehension of good and evil is given in the running of the blood." I went back to the desk, and with this line, the poem flowed. For months I thought of that line as a gift from the gods.

Then, reading Milosz one afternoon, I saw that the line was his—the first line in his poem "One More Day," a poem I didn't even remember reading. How could this have happened? If I hadn't picked up the book, maybe I never would have known that the line repeating through my poem wasn't mine, but one that had been created by someone else.

In my series, I had felt that one poem was touched by Gabriel's tone, another by Richard's. I'd decided that this was okay; the speaker of each poem was so clearly different from Gabriel or Richard, and I had used nothing factual about either man. But this truth of Elmo's was different.

I sat in my rocker and worried about the nature of poetry. Milosz had also written, in *"Ars Poetica?,"* "The purpose of poetry is to remind us/how difficult it is to remain just one person,/for our house is open, there are no keys in the doors,/and invisible guests come in and out at will." This truth is what I loved about poetry, and what made the form dangerous.

"Ars Poetica?" recognized that "In the very essence of poetry there is something indecent:/a thing is brought forth which we didn't know we had in us. . . ." Milosz was referring to beings within, but Elmo was the one who came through my poem, unbidden.

Milosz continued: "That's why poetry is rightly said to be dictated by a daimonion,/though it's an exaggeration to maintain that he must be an angel . . . " and, "What reasonable man would like to be a city of demons,/who behave as if they were at home, speak in many tongues,/and, who, not satisfied with stealing his lips or hand,/work at changing his destiny for their convenience?"

Not I, not at this moment. At night's darkest hour, I sat in my rocking chair frightened by how easily other beings spoke through my poems. Elmo had told me something that was crucial to his ability to keep his humanity alive in prison, a place where the odds were stacked against such survival. There had been not one shred of motive inside me that desired to abuse Elmo's trust, and still I had.

So I wanted to stop writing. Which was the second strand of pain swirling inside me. For besides the hurt I'd inadvertently caused Elmo, I recognized that Elmo's voice sounded just like the familiar voice of Doubt. The angry tone of Elmo's words echoed that of my lifelong internal critic, the one who managed to find a multiplicity of ways to let me know I had no right to speak, the one who, all through my younger years, made me discount my own point of view. Tonight Elmo's voice had sounded just like the voice that, my whole life, tried to silence my own. Elmo's powerful voice was making me ask once again: His need or mine?

As I sat in my rocker, I tried to find what, in those years, I continually hungered for: that vantage point from which our needs coexisted. From this viewpoint I could see that Elmo and I shared a strong human desire to be closer, to know each other, to become friends, and all this was controlled by prison rules. Spoon and I needed human connection, too, and we had found a way to be close that didn't resist prison protocol. Elmo's righteous energy wouldn't accept the limits Spoon and I managed to live with. So I always experienced Elmo's insistence that we were two human beings desiring real communication as an in-my-face challenge.

But as night moved toward dawn, I saw Elmo didn't mean to challenge me. I had handed him the role of censor when, in fact, what my body had interpreted as attacks, Elmo intended as invitations. Elmo *wanted* me to respond with my truth, to do my part to bridge the gap between us—to speak, always to speak. What I perceived as a roadblock, he intended as an avenue for approach.

By the time the late winter morning broke over the hills I could see from our window, I knew I could rise from the rocking chair and reenter San Quentin without dread. I stood up, made Sara a smoothie for breakfast, and got ready for work.

Jim was away for two days of meetings, so I walked across the Plaza and into an empty office. I never figured out how news traveled so quickly in the small town of San Quentin, but as soon as I unlocked the door, my students appeared, one by one, to tell me what they thought I should know.

Some men were sad I'd felt hurt and wanted to see how I was feeling this morning, some wanted to give me a lecture about how I listened too respectfully to outrageous positions, some wanted to bad-mouth Elmo. As usual, I saw each man as a complex human being filled with a universe of thoughts and motives. But as I listened first to one man, then to another—that shifting point of view I'd asked for—I picked out the thread of a subtext.

For the eighteen months that our class had been meeting, most of my students—Coties, Elmo, Glenn, Spoon—had been black. Chicano Angel, white Richard, and Japanese-Anglo Gabriel fit into the group just fine. Most of the other white men who had attended class briefly, however, left after only a few sessions. I didn't live in a cell block or work out on the yard, so I didn't know intimately the racism that permeated prison culture. I assumed race was part of the reason these white men left class, though, because more than one had told me I brought in too many African American guest artists. I wanted every man to feel comfortable in our class and was conscious of balance—racial, sexual, subject matter, tone—but I wasn't going to stop bringing in black poets. I felt bad, of course, when a man chose to stop attending class. But I realized that I could not please everyone and each man had to be free to make his own choices.

Angel had been paroled, and Richard had transferred, and the previous night, the core group of blacks-plus-Gabriel had been joined by a whole new mix: two more black men, one Native American, and four whites. Because we'd hardly met as a class, I hadn't had an opportunity to notice how this new group would function. As I listened to first one man, then another, in the office that Tuesday, I realized that at least some of the "pointed and ugly" emotions I'd sensed but been unable to name the night before stemmed largely from racial hatred.

Over the following year, the racism in class would increase, and I'd never find a way to address it. During that time, more than one man would come within a hair's breadth of calling me a "nigger-lover," and the light, easy mood we'd shared for eighteen months would become edgy and sharp, until again, most of the white men decided to quit, leaving our class preponderantly black.

When Luis walked into the building, I went to his office and told him what had happened.

"Now you understand why we're wary of Elmo?"

I nodded and began a "Yes, but . . . "

Luis raised his palm. "No one's saying he's not smart."

I shrugged and didn't get into the fine points, for Luis clearly wanted to give me a lecture.

"I've been watching you, and Henry's been watching you, and you are handling yourself in a very professional manner. You're doing nothing wrong."

Again I started to speak.

"Listen, you have to know that you're a woman working in a male institution. You're a free person in a world of animosity you'll never come close to understanding. And not every inmate is wrapped too tight. You have to get straight with the fact that some incident could occur out on the yard and it could be related to you, though you'd done nothing to feed it. That could happen; someone could get killed. Even if you're doing your best to be conscious. And anyone, inmate or staff, out of spite or whatever, could accuse you of whatever he wants to.

"If you're not willing to accept this, you'd better walk out the door now and not come back to the prison. You're no longer in Berkeley or some revolutionary paradise. This is San Quentin; make peace with the fact."

I'd asked to stand on ground where I could see the whole composed of one truth next to another, but that morning had been like a point-of-view sequence run at fast-forward. For three hours, one man, then another, told me *his* view of what had come down and how *he* thought I should respond. Now Luis had added his voice to the chorus.

I walked back to the Arts-in-Corrections office and laid my head on the desk. Manny stood in the door and asked if he could enter. Though Manny hadn't remained in our class, he was a clerk in Operations, and we often talked. He had come to prison as a young man strung out on drugs and had been scared to his senses by all the guns going off. Now Manny's only addiction was running. He could run six miles in thirty-eight minutes. "Not bad for a forty-six-year-old former drug fiend," Manny said with pride.

Manny sat down and responded to what must have been my look of exhaustion. He wanted to make me feel better, that was clear, but there was nothing to say.

"I just want to understand," I told Manny. "I guess I must believe that if I pay enough attention, understanding will follow."

Manny shook his head. "This is prison," he said. "There's no way to understand."

Most of my students dropped by over the following days, but not Elmo. I rarely saw Elmo between class sessions, so this was not unusual. Still, I experienced his absence as a gap. I longed to leap over this gulf, to find a way to erase separation. But I knew I had to be patient and wait until Elmo was ready to forgive me and until I was sure I wouldn't let whatever he said shut me up.

I anticipated Monday's class with both excitement and dread, not knowing what to expect. My friend Kiva—a poet from Elk, a tiny town twenty miles north of Point Arena—was scheduled to be a guest artist. I thought about asking Kiva to postpone her visit, but decided that having a guest, especially one whose poems and presence were as solid and steady as Kiva's, would most likely be good for us all. I called Kiva to explain the situation, and she agreed to accompany me into the unknown.

Before Kiva's reading, though, I felt I had to say something. But what?

When I asked James, he said, "Whatever you do, don't cry. That would split us in two."

"But I don't know if I can. Not cry, I mean."

"You can't cry, that's all there is to it," James's gentle eyes fixed me. "Welcome to prison," I heard for what seemed like the hundredth time that week.

....

Over the weekend, I took Spoon as my model. When the Point Arena kids' poems had been taken from him, Spoon responded by writing a poem. I worked on a piece that began:

> *My whole life I have feared being strangled.*
> *When someone gets near my throat, I bolt . . .*

and ended:

> *When I was fourteen, that whole year,*
> *I had one strep throat, then another.*
> *For weeks at a time, my throat tightened and burned.*
> *It hurt too much to talk.*
>
> *Now I'm forty. I still want to lie*
> *without moving so I won't cough,*
> *to drink tea and be quiet.*
> *But I know I was put here to speak,*
> *and though it still hurts,*
> *I'm going to open my mouth,*
> *let the words out.*

When I walked into the office on Monday, Jim greeted me with a weary smile. "I just got a call from Lukman," Jim told me. "You'd better sit down."

Lukman managed the Artist in Social Institutions section of the California Arts Council residency program and was, therefore, in charge of my work on the grant.

"He's coming to observe your class tonight," Jim delivered.

"What?" I protested.

Jim shrugged. "He's in the Bay Area doing site visits."

"Did you tell him about last week?"

"I told him he might witness an interesting class. You can fill him in on whatever details you want when he gets here."

Finally, I just laughed. My anticipation of class seemed as amped as it could get, and for the moment, this new twist struck me as funny.

I met Lukman at East Gate and escorted him inside. I barely knew Lukman, but I'd resigned myself to the fact that this near stranger who had some control over my project was about to join me in an intimate encounter of some sort. As we walked through Scope Gate and Count Gate, I gave Lukman the short version.

All twelve men showed up to class. Kiva took a seat next to me, and Lukman found a chair off to the side. By now, the only nervousness I felt about Lukman's visit was that my students would think he was there to monitor them rather than me. So, although I wasn't sure they'd believe me, I began class by saying, "He's here to evaluate me. This has nothing to do with any of you."

I said my poem to a room full of eyes and no words, then introduced Kiva.

"It was a song heard deep/moving across the plains," Kiva read, and "Something buried deep/turns over."

We all settled into Kiva's world of land and spirit. "With these words," Kiva read, "I redeem the human body./I claim this blood/ this womb,/and bear it witness."

After Kiva's reading, the men asked her questions. Elmo, usually the one to most fully engage any guest artist, instead sat steadily writing. The room filled with Kiva's quiet responses, then stilled. I asked each man to choose one of his poems to share with Kiva. When it was Elmo's turn, he read from the sheet on which he'd been writing that evening. "This Thing Inside of Me" was the poem's title.

How can I give this thing a name?
This thing inside of me
This thing I feel
It is a hungry thing
And my greatest fear
is that it wants to consume me.

I fight this thing
Not with any weapon I can describe
but it is a battle just the same
The part of me that matters most
could fit into a spoon
or be so vast
that it "surrounds" rather than "fits into"
anything
The part of me that matters most
is what fears this thing.

The part of me that matters most
hides like a rabbit inside my wolf body
My flesh is the sentinel that wards off
all intruders
All except
this thing
This thing which has taken root
so near my sacred garden
This hungry weed
whose roots are entangled in mine
tempts me
evokes my anger
makes me more like the animal
I try not to be.

How do I fight this thing?
This crafty thing
which moves in and out of me
like a tide
moves through me

with the force of radiation
deadly but unseen
How do I fight this thing?
And how much of me shall remain
when the battle is finally over?

seven

Long-Term, In-Depth

"Long-term, in-depth," the Arts Council wrote, describing the grants that it gave; "long-term, in-depth" is what I had asked for. Now, as often happened when I got what I wished for, the gift seemed a mixed blessing. All the teaching I'd done up to this point in my life had been as an outsider coming to students for brief and intense stints. In the bright light of that sharing, my students and I knew only the best about each other.

For the first time in my work life I was there, as Lynnelle had put it, for the long haul. My students and I now shared not only smiles and good vibes, but a fuller range of emotions. We shared disappointment, as when the Point Arena kids' poems were taken from Spoon, and pain, such as the hurt I felt at Elmo's anger and his feeling of betrayal. We were coming to know each other, as one of the men put it, "warts and all."

In class one Monday night I talked of my idea for our next publication project: a series of chapbooks. Each student would design

124

and assemble a small book of his poems, and I'd distribute these as a series.

Coties asked how long each book would take to create. "Will it take a month of Mondays?" he asked. And Month of Mondays became the name of our press.

....

Later that week I sat at my desk and turned around to see Gabriel standing at the office door.

"Do you have time to look at a new poem?" he asked. "I want to include it in my chapbook."

Jim was on the phone and Lynnelle was at her desk, so I rose and walked into the hall and sat down at the table placed there.

"*Ani ohev otach*," Gabriel said.

I was startled. Gabriel had just said "I love you."

"I'm learning Hebrew," he told me. "I know the feminine endings are different. How would *you* say that line?"

Ani ohevet etchah. I knew how to say it, but I doubted Gabriel was asking me for language instruction. There was no way I was going to speak those words to Gabriel in any tongue.

"Let's see the poem, Gabriel."

I read the title, "Below the Waterline," and the epigraph: "The drowned man's hand tells a story of life below the waterline." The poem ended:

I see the waterline
everyday, with eyes clenched tight
I struggle for each live breath
between iron bars, and
grasp the sky
above a concrete sea

So please!
don't reproach me
when I reach for the world
reflected in your eyes

for I live
below the waterline

The poem's descriptions were gorgeous: "Just when these wrinkles cover the flesh/cobalt blue," "See fingers clutch at the clouds," "hunger etched in the eyes." I knew that Gabriel was talking to me, telling me that, given his incarcerated reality, of course he was going to "reach out for the world/reflected in [my] eyes."

While I sat there facing the usual dilemma Gabriel posed—how to honor both the poem and Gabriel's human need for love, while at the same time being clear that I in no way reciprocated that love—I heard a loud "Boo!" right behind me. I turned around in instinctual fright and saw one of the clerks, a kid barely older than Sara, giggling over his success in surprising me.

Gabriel stared at me with his piercing gaze. "You don't have to be scared. I'll always protect you."

Gevalt, I thought in Yiddish, not Hebrew. *Oi gevalt.*

In September, a few of us Arts-in-Corrections folk were gathered in a conference room in Sacramento. We were there to meet the new director of the California Department of Corrections, James Rowland. We had just finished lunch, and Jim Carlson was teaching us all to juggle. A few dozen cascading square beanbags filled the room, when in walked a kind-looking, round man. Bill Cleveland's face shifted between desperation and mirth, but Rowland just laughed, "Well, juggling is the basic skill required in my job, too."

We all scrambled to sit down and compose ourselves. Once we were settled, Rowland began with a practiced public speaker's opening joke, then quickly got serious.

"When I ask the public if it believes in rehabilitation," he said, "they answer, 'no.' But when I ask, 'Do you think we should teach illiterate inmates to read?' most often they say 'yes.' So I don't use the word 'rehabilitation'; instead I talk about increasing the likelihood that men and women in prison can return to our communities as productive citizens.

"I'm well aware that no matter what programs we offer, there are people in prison who aren't going to change; they're simply not ready. I know there are others who will turn their lives around, even if we offer them nothing.

"But there's a vast majority in the middle who will change if they encounter the right program. It's going to be a different one for each person. For some it's AA, for some playing piano, for some college classes, for some," he indicated the beanbags piled at the table's center, "it might even be juggling. So I take it as part of the department's task to offer as wide a range of programs as we can, because each one is likely to make a positive impact on some inmate."

We artists sat stunned. This Republican-appointed CDC director was saying exactly what we had always said! Rowland talked to us of his belief that men and women in prison must take responsibility for the consequences of their crimes. He asked us to consider the ways the work we did with our students might further this goal. How could inmates making art serve the larger community? How might we address victims' needs? How might we provide public service opportunities for our prison students?

During the drive back to San Quentin, Jim moaned. If Rowland had been heading the department only a few months before, Spoon might still have those poems the kids in Point Arena wrote him. If Rowland had been director in February, Jim and I might have been encouraged to pursue the very prisoner-youngster poetry exchange we'd instead been prohibited from exploring.

Rowland's stewardship *had* led the warden to consider Jim's proposal for a San Quentin production of *Waiting for Godot*. When Jim had suggested that we have three performances for outside audiences, who would be asked to make a contribution to Bay Area victim/witness programs, the warden had been pleased: This was exactly the kind of project his new boss desired.

....

One morning Spoon sat in Lynnelle's chair talking to me. "But," he said, his voice very low, "Do you really think I can do it?"

Jan, the director from Sweden, wanted Spoon to play Pozzo, and for weeks Jim and I had been urging him to accept the role. Even on first reading, Spoon loved Beckett's language. But he wondered if he had it in him to roar, really roar, on stage, in front of an audience.

I'd sent Jan copies of Spoon's chapbook. When he briefly returned to San Quentin in August, Jan told Spoon that he had placed the book in the Nobel Library in Stockholm, had the poems read over Swedish radio, and had taken a copy to Paris, where Beckett now kept it close by him, on his bedside table.

The sudden gift of an international audience and of one very eminent reader was amazing to Spoon—as it would be, of course, to any poet. Jan told stories of the wide attention he was sure the San Quentin production of *Godot* would garner. Spoon was intrigued. Still, he worried, "What if I can't find the realness? What if I can't make it real?"

Jan was due back to the prison in early December. Meanwhile, Ralph and his best buddy, Mike, were set to play Gogo and Didi. The two men rehearsed every chance they got, approaching their roles with the rollicking humor of their real-life friendship. Gabriel was going to join the cast, too. Jan wanted Gabriel as Lucky, the near-silent one at the bound end of Pozzo's taut rope.

....

"Jim," I burst out as soon as I entered the office, "look at this!" As usual, my excitement made me oblivious to the I'm-up-to-my-eyeballs look on Jim's face. He graciously looked at the article I shoved under his nose:

Bill Irwin will [tread] the boards with Steve Martin and Robin Williams at New York's Lincoln Center in Samuel Beckett's absurdist classic "Waiting for Godot." Mike Nichols directs. Martin will play Vladimir and Williams Estragon. F. Murray Abraham is cast as Pozzo and Irwin as Lucky.

I spent the morning on the phone, tracking down addresses for Williams and Irwin. These two stars had lived in San Francisco and were, I figured, the ones most likely to be back in town in the near future. I wanted to write, letting them know of our project and extending invitations to visit San Quentin rehearsals. By noon, I'd taken two letters to the Mail Room, the first stop on their way to New York.

On a Wednesday afternoon the week before Thanksgiving, I sat laughing loudly with a group of ten men in our usual classroom. Spoon was there, and Gabriel, Ralph, Chris, and Carl from our poetry class. Danny, chosen by Jan to play the part of the boy, had joined us, as had four others. The room was uncharacteristically dark as we all watched Laurel and Hardy do pratfalls on the video monitor.

We were halfway through an eight-week course for those who wanted to learn more about Beckett's work. We'd just talked about Laurel and Hardy, about how their look and their particular brand of humor served as one model for Didi and Gogo.

Joseph Miksak, who played Pozzo in the San Francisco Actor's Workshop 1957 production, had come in with photos and stories. We'd watched Billie Whitelaw in *Rockaby* on video. In the weeks ahead, other actors and directors who had performed Beckett's work were scheduled to visit. But on this particular afternoon, we sat in that dungeon-y basement watching Laurel and Hardy, and laughing.

In late November, I walked out at lunchtime to buy a small salad. Although the prison staff's snack bar had a linoleum and plastic decor and served sloppy joes and saltines instead of portobello

mushrooms and focaccia bread, the glass that ran halfway around
the curved room's circumference had a view any toney Bay Area
restaurant would covet. I sat eating wilted iceberg lettuce, looking
out at the bay and the cove's rocky beach. The Richmond–San
Rafael bridge seemed a stately line drawing against the wash of
November's gray sky.

"Mind if I join you?"

My open palm indicated the modular chair next to my own, and
Suzan sat down.

Suzan, a lieutenant ready to become a program administrator,
was one of the very few people on staff I'd spent time with away
from the prison. Suzan grew up in Berkeley, knew how to be both
professional and kind, and, people said, we looked alike. Suzan had
come to my apartment for brunch; we'd hiked one Sunday after-
noon on Mt. Tam.

The previous April, when Gary Glassman had come to make a
video of my students saying their poems, Spoon had been rolled
up. Suzan had instituted a quick investigation, confirmed Spoon
had done nothing out of line, and had arranged his release in time
for our filming. I felt I could ask Suzan's advice on prison matters
without her overreacting. And, since she was sitting right here at
my side, I now asked her about Gabriel.

"You know, I'm not one to panic," she said after I'd described
my two years of trying to dodge Gabriel's obsession, "but this guy
is serious business." I knew Suzan had once been the object of
Gabriel's attentions, so I listened particularly carefully to what she
had to say.

"I tried just what you're trying: clear refusals, giving advice.
Nothing worked. Finally I had to stop speaking to him. Not a
word. Just like that. I walked away whenever he approached me."

Suzan insisted I follow her to Records, a long, second-floor of-
fice where every prisoner's file was kept. I hadn't been to Records
before, had never even thought about reading a student's file. Jim
didn't read files either, although now prison officials told him he

had to check the records of all the men who wanted to be in *Godot*, since they were likely to have a great deal of contact with the public. Jim hadn't gotten to Gabriel's file yet.

When I looked up from reading the file, Suzan just nodded. "See, he repeats the same pattern with every woman he falls for. He's dangerous, Judith; you have to take care."

I walked back to Operations feeling about as gray and cloud-laden as the sky over my head. I started talking to Jim as soon as I closed our office door. Then we pondered: Should we bar Gabriel from my class? We accepted Suzan's assessment of Gabriel's obsessive blindness and the danger this might lead to, but Gabriel hadn't actually *done* anything wrong. In fact, Gabriel was one of Arts-in-Corrections' most supportive and helpful students. "Boy," Jim sighed, "this is a tough one."

Jim went across the hall to talk with Denise, the woman who had taken Luis's place as community resources manager when Luis transferred to the new prison in San Diego. Denise and Jim decided that Gabriel, who had not crossed the line into the zone of punishable behavior, could remain in arts classes, but that we'd find ways to be particularly careful. Jim had a talk with Weichel and told him to make sure I was never left alone with Gabriel.

The next time Gabriel came to the office, he told Jim of his feelings. "Look, you're a poet," Jim responded. "Put your feelings in poems. Keep a diary. Use your emotions as fuel for your work."

A Bay Area radio newscaster, Scoop Nisker, had visited our class a number of times, sharing a lesson on haiku during one visit, and playing a tape of Jack Kerouac reading from his work as Steve Allen played piano on another occasion. Toward the end of 1987, Scoop returned to make an audiotape of my students saying their poems.

Scoop had asked each man to prepare a few introductory words about what writing meant to him. Spoon said, "Writing for me is like an oasis in the desert; it quenches my thirst." Coties told whoever would hear the tape, "I really respect my poems because they exemplify the realness in me, that part that no one else seems to know." As was his custom, Chris let no one off any hook, introducing himself as "presently in the concentration camp that's known as San Quentin."

The day Scoop played the tape on radio station KPFA, Arts-in-Corrections was flooded with phone calls. One man said that he'd had to pull his car over to the side of the road in response to hearing a poem a new student had written to his mother. The man told me he couldn't stop crying; the poem made him ache for his own son, who had gotten into trouble but was such a good kid at heart.

My heart was full: My students were being heard all over the Bay Area. These San Quentin poets were, at least for this moment, included in the world beyond prison, affecting listeners with the words they'd crafted to shape their emotions.

....

For the third morning in a row, I handed Jim the *Doonesbury* strip as soon as I walked in the door. For the third morning, Jim laughed as Zonker and Mike—decked out as Didi and Gogo—searched all over for the Mario Cuomo who might, or might not, announce his presidential candidacy.

On this third day of Trudeau's "Waiting for Mario" vignette, we expected the arrival of our own Godot at any moment. Jan's plane had landed and he was set to spend the next seven months preparing San Quentin's 1988 production of *Waiting for Godot*.

When Jan finally walked through the door, he was confronted with the news that Mike had decided not to play Vladimir after all. He had told Jim that he'd been pulled in by Ralph's exuberance, but that he really didn't want to spend the next half year of his life rehearsing and performing.

Jan was distraught. For Jim, though, this defection, as well as the stack of memos he'd already written—memos for Arts-in-Corrections paid positions that would allow the cast to rehearse all day as their prison jobs; memos for permission to use San Quen-

132

tin's video studio for rehearsals; memos that would gain entry to the prison for a slew of Swedish photographers and journalists we'd been told would descend over the course of the next months—was business as usual.

Jan spent a few days wandering around the prison looking at faces. He asked Chris to read for him. The image of Chris's tall, dark, contained being next to Ralph's bouncy, white stoutness pleased the director.

I lobbied for Chris, whom I liked more and more. I knew his constant political consciousness-raising got on some nerves, but although I agreed that Chris's speeches could sound like harangues, I'd come to admire how in prison he had informed himself about the history of his African American people and about inequality in this country, and I admired him for taking on the task of educating others.

Chris wanted to be in the play, but his "walk smooth" demeanor didn't reveal this to the director. Jan—the complete opposite of "cool"—loved drama and heightened emotions. His eyes turned watery and his whole face assumed a studied expression of pain every time he saw a guard leading a handcuffed man across the Upper Yard: "Pozzo and Lucky," Jan sighed, deeply enough to carry clear to the back of any theater.

The men who repeated Jan's lines back to him—"This play is my diary"—were the ones whose interest Jan believed. But such sycophancy was light-years away from Chris Brown's style.

Jim told Chris that Jan needed to be convinced of his desire to play Didi. Chris listened. Chris was serving a life sentence, which meant he had to appear repeatedly before the Board of Prison Terms to argue the case for his parole. By the end of 1987, Chris had already served close to fifteen years and had been to the board many times. A prisoner would spend months preparing for the board and those months must have invited both the greatest of hopes and the deepest of doubts. Chris knew well about that endless waiting for what may never come depicted in *Godot*. Chris told

Jim of these repeated rejections by the board and said, "I've learned not to get too excited until something is real." Still, Chris made an effort to express interest in language Jan would understand.

But Ralph and Chris just did not get along. Ralph was one of those who hated Chris's insistence on giving a political analysis of every situation, and he made this dislike apparent. In class, Ralph often offered what he thought of as neutral observations, while he charged Chris with speaking from a racial perspective. When I pointed out that Ralph, as a white male, was allowed to perceive his views as "neutral," while those with less power were seen as representing "special interests," Ralph would shake his head in disgust.

Ralph was not happy about the prospect of performing *Godot* with Chris, and he searched the blocks for a Didi he would rather work with. He soon brought Twin to read for Jan. Twin was also African American, also a physical contrast to Ralph, and although reading a play script was unfamiliar to Twin, Jan liked the man's presence.

Of course, I was rooting for Chris, but finally, Jan threw up his hands. "It simply won't work. Didi and Gogo have to put their arms around each other, they have to embrace. Ralph can't even look Chris in the face."

Jan asked me to accompany him to West Block to break the news to Chris. So on a late afternoon very near Christmas, we climbed up to the fifth tier.

Jan launched into an elaborate explanation, but I watched Chris quickly get the subtext. Chris knew what lay beneath Jan's decision, but he never said one single word against Ralph. Instead, he gracefully accepted being passed over and wished Jan best of luck with the play.

I knew I'd just witnessed a class act. As Jan walked away, though, I was stuck in one of those San Quentin moments: I wanted to acknowledge the admiration I felt for the way Chris had pulled off the previous fifteen minutes; at the same time, I was concerned that if I said anything, I might undercut the dignity Chris had achieved. I tried to find the right balance, but the words, to my ears, sounded pretty silly. Once again Chris was gracious, focusing on my intention and not my sputtering speech.

On a Monday night after the New Year, I talked to the men in the poetry class about my idea for our next Month of Mondays publication: a series of poetry broadsides. In my attempt to make my program design as apparent as possible, I wrote figures on the chalkboard to let the men know the details of the budget my grant provided.

Chris, in a tone that was more playful than confrontational, asked, "Why do you need to pay guest artists? If they're sincere, they'll want to come in." The rest of the men joined in. I knew I was being teased, was being sweetly asked to acknowledge the truth: Despite the democratic look of those figures on the board, *I* was the one making the decisions.

But I was not in a mood to be teased; I was exhausted. *Godot* had expanded my twenty-hours-per-week grant by at least another twenty unpaid hours, and on this particular night, all the work was getting me down. So I blew up. I said nothing coherent, but I certainly spewed anger around the classroom.

By this point, my students and I had seen each other in many different situations. Just a few weeks earlier, a couple of the men, noticing how tired I was, had received Jim's permission to plan a party for me. Officer Weichel, in on the surprise, came to our classroom and announced an electrical problem; he said we had to move to another room. When I walked into that new room, I was stunned to see a huge banner and food and cards the men had made for me.

During another class session, I was talking about the ballad structure. Someone asked me to give an example, and I started to sing "Jesse James," pointing out the song's abcb rhyme scheme and its common meter alternation of a four-beat and a three-beat line.

I had always longed to be a singer. My Aunty Emma was a professional, my mother had a beautiful voice, and my sister directed a choral group and taught music. I, however, took after my father, who had been asked to silently mouth the words during grammar school singing classes. Still, I felt so close to my students that particular night, I let myself share even my off-key, rickety voice. I was shy and embarrassed, and that was okay.

But that Monday evening in January 1988, I was angry, and anger is what I shared with my students. The next day, Gabriel stood at the door to our office and told Jim, "Wow! It was like we pushed one button and her whole panel went off!"

The actor Bill Irwin had responded to the letter I'd sent him, and in early February, he visited San Quentin. Bill joined Jan, Jim, and me for one of those lettuce-and-saltine luncheons at the snack bar. Jan, sick with the flu, went back to his San Francisco flat, and I escorted Bill inside to meet the cast.

Bill knew very well about the 1957 San Francisco Actor's Workshop production at San Quentin. He'd worked for some years with the workshop's director, Herbert Blau, who, Bill said, spoke more frequently of the San Quentin performance than of the one in Brussels at the World's Fair.

When we were settled, Ralph asked about rehearsals for the *Godot* that Bill was appearing in at Lincoln Center. Bill responded, "We haven't even set the date of production yet; everyone's schedule is so tight."

"You know," Bill looked at Ralph, Twin, Spoon, Gabriel, and Danny, each man in turn, and said, "I envy your six months of five-day-a-week rehearsals."

"Yes, but you don't have to worry about lockdowns or transfers," Gabriel replied.

"That's true," Bill nodded. The few moments of silence that followed held our mutual acknowledgment of the vast gap between conditions under which the Lincoln Center and San Quentin casts approached *Godot*.

"Your lives at San Quentin are very different from mine," Bill said, "and your working process will be different from ours on a commercial production, but here are a couple of thoughts, for whatever they're worth. I haven't done too much in my life other than work in the theater. It's very hard work, but for me, the joy and satisfaction of working on a play are thinking about it—whatever the play is—and trying things, experimenting with things, repeating them over and over until they tell something about my life.

"You are interdependent when you do a play. The other actors depend on you, but sometimes the best thing you can do is surprise them a little bit and see what it gives them. You have a good director, so you can count on him to rein you in if you go too far off the beaten path."

The men listened, nodding, and then Ralph asked, "How are you approaching Lucky?"

"I don't know exactly." Bill rose as he spoke, and his arms, legs, torso, and bent head searched for movements that might reveal the Lucky he sensed. "I see him as someone who was once an *artiste*, a thinker.

"I once saw an old Chinese man on TV." Bill bent his knees and turned. "Maybe ten years ago, I can't quite remember. I'd like to use what he did."

Gabriel watched Bill's approximate sequence, stood up himself, and leaned into movement. "You mean this?" Gabriel asked.

"Exactly," Bill said as he mirrored Gabriel's gestures.

The men resumed talking, but for a long time I was still. For here I was, sitting on the floor, leaning against the brick wall that once marked the literal hole—that dungeon whose cells were niches cut into stone with no light and only the foulest of air—watching a masterful mime I'd admired for years learn a movement from a San Quentin lifer.

....

The following day I walked into San Quentin particularly happy. Saturday would be my forty-first birthday, and I felt, as they say, in the prime of my life. I loved my work at the prison, loved Sara, loved the man in my life; I was giving many readings of my San Quentin poems throughout the Bay Area, had recently had two articles published, and had begun work on a manual for artists working in prison that Bill Cleveland had hired me to research and write. Sara was healthy and happy and would graduate high school in June. She and I were planning our last-trip-of-her-childhood to New York City for spring vacation.

I walked into the prison with an extra-rich batch of chocolate chip cookies because there was to be a potluck at lunchtime in Operations. By eleven we were shoving tables together and gathering chairs from every office to set around them. By half past eleven I was sitting with Associate Warden Tabash and two secretaries, Dale and Pat. Between bites, Dale turned toward me. She was the only other woman I'd seen at San Quentin who wore Birkenstock sandals, as I did, the only other woman I saw run around in stocking feet, as I did, as she moved from her desk to the photocopy machine. "So, Judith," Dale teased. "In the '6os, were you a real hippie?"

"Not a hippie, exactly," I began, wondering if I should complete my response. "More like a radical." I knew "radical" was the enemy—especially at San Quentin, with its George Jackson history. But Henry, Dale, and Pat merely raised their eyebrows and went on eating.

After the potluck, I walked outside the gates of the prison on my way to the warden's office to give him the last of our chapbooks. As I walked through Count Gate, I thought, once again, of how strange it was that radical-vegetarian-poet-me should feel so at home here at San Quentin. Strange, but that February afternoon, very true.

The warden took the chapbooks I brought him, then said, "Good that you're here. I heard something I want to check out. Seems an inmate spoke with the head of our San Quentin Citizens Advisory Council. Said he thinks of you all the time; said he's in love with you. She brought this information to me."

I looked out the large window behind the warden's desk at the castlelike turrets of the prison beyond. I stared at the oak veneer paneled walls with their plaques, certificates, framed photos, and awards. Then I turned to the warden and told him the story.

"We'll have to roll him up," he said, "and check this out." The warden lifted the handset from the telephone on the large walnut table at which we sat. "We'll get the squad on it."

"You look pretty shaken," he said to me as he hung up the phone.

I knew the warden was reading every nuance of my response, but I sat with my usual mixed feelings and had no mask to put on. "Well, of course I've hated his not listening to my repeated 'No,' but I don't think he's ever even had a write-up. And he's in *Godot*. Just yesterday he impressed a performer as fine as Bill Irwin."

The warden shook his head. "Listen, you know what? Poets aren't the only ones with feelings, but I'll tell you, I'm not carrying anyone's anxiety but my own."

He rose to dismiss me. "Write me a memo giving me all the details. Bring it in tomorrow, and we'll take it from there."

It was after half past three, and I knew Jim had left for the day. The last thing I wanted was to go back inside where the squad was that minute most likely escorting Gabriel in handcuffs. So I followed the barbed-wire fence that borders the prison along its western edge until I came to the Valley—the area of on-site staff housing—hoping Suzan would be home from her second-watch shift. As I walked, I heard gunshot: guards at the rifle range nearby.

"Good," Suzan said when she heard what had happened. "Judith, he's in here for life; he's going to come into contact with lots of women. I'm glad this is going to become part of his record."

I nodded, but felt little conviction. All I wanted was to curl up with a pillow over my head, pretending none of this had happened; instead, I spent the evening writing the memo the warden had asked for.

The next day, Associate Warden King called me into her office and asked for a full report. It took about two seconds to realize that Gabriel wasn't the only one under investigation: I was, too.

This made sense to me. I'd seen free women lead prisoners on and had heard dozens of stories of female staff or volunteers discovered having sex with a prisoner in some storeroom. So I thought it was reasonable that staff would make sure I hadn't been in some way complicit. This acknowledgment didn't make me like the questions Meredith King now asked me, however, or the scrutiny I was apparently under. Oh, so *this* is the kind of situation that leads one to "walk smooth," I thought.

Even though prison is an established institution, it is also a community, and a particular kind of community at that: a neighborhood, a small town. Everyone watches everyone else all the time. In Point Arena, if some Annie was seen with some Billy more than once, the town soon considered the two as an "item." Annie might have been consulting Billy for advice about pruning fruit trees, but in Point Arena, appearance was all.

At San Quentin, too, perception was nine-tenths of the truth. So no matter what facts any investigation of me revealed, I knew my culpability would depend largely on how I comported myself as I walked through the grounds these next days.

When the squad cleared out Gabriel's cell, they found the diary Jim had advised Gabriel, the writer, to keep. In it he chronicled his every encounter with me, those conversations that had half driven me nuts, those times when I'd said something like, "Gabriel, this is your fantasy," and he had responded, "I'm in prison; fantasy is all I've got," and I'd accepted that, well, this was true in its way. Or the times when I'd told him I didn't return his feelings and never would, and he'd told me, "You can't say 'never,' you can't know the future," and, of course, I had to acknowledge this fact. I could see why Suzan had finally simply stopped talking to Gabriel.

Sexual desire and the longing to be emotionally close to another creature are part of the human experience. A man or woman in prison doesn't stop being human, and so doesn't stop desiring closeness. "I have a poem," prison poet after poet would tell me. "You can read it, but don't show it to anyone else." Most often these poems were love poems. Not the "You're my woman" love poems they read in class with comfort, but more of a "Baby, I need you" aching kind of poem.

Many of these men had been locked up so long, there was not a real woman in their lives. If there was not, they wrote to the memory of Woman. Remembering Woman and Love seemed to help polish that jewel in the left side of each chest. Every one of my students wrote, at least sometimes, from his vulnerable, gentle, and soft heart, but very few were willing to share these poems with their fellow prisoners. The harsh world they lived in convinced many men they were the only ones expressing such softness.

The world of corrections views any intimate human exchange—not only sex, but also friendship, political comradeship, or a variety of other forms of bonding—between prisoners and staff as dangerous. Whether this concern originated from a view of inmates as animals whose only reason for wanting to be close with an employee would be to manipulate that employee, or from the view that the institution itself needed protection from the human instincts of both prisoners *and* staff, or from some wholly different motivation, I did not know. The way I heard some staff describe the conundrum went something like this: "Hell, if I were an inmate, I'd go after whatever I could. That's just human nature." They described their jobs as what sounded to me like a parental strategy of setting limits. I often heard such staff members speak of this game as one in which no one—neither inmate nor guard—took any fair action personally. Instead, everyone involved did what he had to do, and then no hard feelings.

I had observed that the most common accusation made against a staff member or other free person in relation to a prisoner in the small town of San Quentin was that he or she was being "overly familiar." The bottom line rule governing the relations of prisoners and staff was paragraph 3400 of the "Director's Rules," a booklet handed to everyone—even teaching artists—working inside prison:

3400 Familiarity
Employees must not engage in undue familiarity with inmates, parolees, or the family and friends of inmates or parolees. Whenever there is a reason for an employee to have personal contact or discussions with an inmate or parolee or the family and friends of inmates and parolees, the employee must maintain a helpful but professional attitude and demeanor. Employees must not discuss their personal affairs with any inmate or parolee.

Of course, paragraph 3400 was not a rule in the same way that "Do not wear blue" was a rule; it was open to interpretation. Paragraph 3400 posed a major professional dilemma for me and for all teaching artists. For how could I do my job, how could I teach poetry, unless I was familiar, unless I insisted, "When you were five, how did your mother walk across the living room floor? When you sat on the porch that summer, how did the concrete feel beneath your bare feet?" "How can you make the word 'oppression' in that line come alive in specifics?" "If you could say whatever you wished to your son, what would it be?" "What do you mean by that word 'pretty?' Blonde hair/blue eyes pretty? Cornrow pretty? Wrinkled-aged-elder pretty?"

I could inundate my students with technical information on metaphoric language, direct imagery, rhythm and meter, line break, and such, but unless I also asked questions such as "When you had that talk with your wife, what was she wearing? How did she move her hands?" I'd be cheating, I would not be sharing poetry.

And, as I'd learned from Elmo that night I'd shared Hikmet's poems, I had no right to ask such questions of my students if I wasn't willing to be intimate, too, revealing my own answers to similar questions. In other words, if I didn't discuss "personal affairs" with my students, I would not be doing my job.

Paragraph 3400 posed a personal dilemma, too. Setting limits was far from my strong suit. When she was fifteen, Sara once told me, "Mom, it's good you had a responsible kid because you'd be a terrible disciplinarian!" Connection, in many forms, was the sensation I lived for, and so I did not naturally know how to assume the "friendly, not friends" tone San Quentin wanted between me and my students.

For example, with Spoon I often felt a spiritual bond so profound, it was as though we'd been fated to meet since birth. I wanted to spend hours "diving," as Spoon put it, into that soul realm we shared. San Quentin made such a possibility highly unlikely!

As for romance, I certainly walked into San Quentin as a sexual being. Sexuality for me had always been intense, driven, and very one-on-one focused. Now, when I'd walk across the Upper Yard or into a cell block, I would encounter hundreds of men denied most forms of sexual expression: There were more raging hormones here than at high school. I knew I had to become less intense *fast*, but I'd never been good at light high school banter. During the years at San Quentin, I laughed at myself and told friends that it took three thousand horny men to teach me to flirt!

Primarily, I tried to channel the energy I felt all around me, as well as the energy I felt within my own body, more toward agape than eros. There *were* erotic moments, though, of course.

One Monday afternoon I walked up to Elmo at the etching press to look at the card he'd just made. Our hands touched, and a sexual spark passed between us.

One evening in class, I'd brought in a tape I'd recorded for the men to listen to as they worked on their chapbooks. I'd recorded individual songs I thought particular men would enjoy—Hank Williams for Carl, Joni Mitchell for Elmo. When Ida Cox broke into "Wild women don't get the blues," Chris asked if that was true. Falling into the raunchy richness of the song, I answered *yes* with all of myself. Elmo and Chris both looked up from their work, surprised.

"*Here's* a whole new Judith," Chris teased.

And for that split second, the current that traveled between us felt fine. But adding that split second to another, and yet another, could lead nowhere but to a broom closet and an illicit quickie, something I didn't want. So it was easy to laugh in an acknowledgment of the sexual moment, then let it go.

Gabriel had been the only student who could not "let it go." It had never seemed inappropriate to me for Gabriel to fall in love with his poetry teacher. His constant attention made me both wary and weary, but until I read his file, I thought Gabriel was simply persistent. Reading that file, then reading the diary the squad took from his cell, I saw how profoundly different Gabriel was from the rest of my students. Although as I write these words, the media seem bent on portraying all prisoners as stalkers, that simply isn't true. My students weren't stalkers. Even Gabriel, who I suppose *was* a stalker, seemed to me to be a man who just got sex wrong. It wasn't my job to make criminal assessments; it was my job to work with human beings. And so I chose to see Gabriel as a person who was so unsure of the responses of the women he was attracted to that he felt he needed to set up a game in which he might deduce these women's feelings.

His diary, begun at Jim's suggestion, revealed Gabriel's obsession and illness. I hated reading this diary, hated knowing how much and in which ways I'd been on his mind. I realized that if Gabriel had not confessed his feelings to someone who was bound to share the information with the warden, I might well have been in physical danger. But Gabriel *had* confessed; Gabriel had written that diary because, as Jim had told him, he *was* a writer. Reading the diary, I could see that Gabriel, himself, was also a victim of his sexual confusion, and because there was so much I liked about Gabriel, this recognition made me very sad.

And speaking of predators, even Gabriel was never as blatant as some male staff. For example, when my students talked to me over our office phone, they teased me about my voice, which they considered sexy. My students teased sweetly, though. It took a male employee I barely knew to put the matter more crudely: "You give good phone," he told me.

Prison officials assigned Gabriel to the Adjustment Center, that building I walked by every time I entered or left the prison. For days I walked through the heavy black door and onto the Plaza hearing Gabriel's voice calling "Judith, Judith" until, finally, his cell was moved to the other side of AC, and a few weeks later, he was transferred to another prison.

eight

"To All Mankind
They Were Addressed":
Godot at San Quentin

I stood in front of East Block's arched entrance, my hand on the buzzer. A guard appeared at the peephole, and I flashed my ID card. I heard the key in the lock, and then the door swung open, and I walked inside what felt like a cavern.

Elmo had been rolled up and placed in a cell in East Block. Word had it he'd be in lockup a long while this time. I had asked for, and received, permission to visit Elmo once a week to bring him poetry papers, look at his poems, chat about class, and lend him an occasional book.

The guard pointed me toward a stack of those turtle-shell vests. I found one that fit well enough and then showed him the scrap of paper on which I'd written Elmo's cell number. Even before looking at this sheet, the officer pointed me toward Yard Side. I saw then that Bay Side was empty, cleared out. The officer told me that the condemned from Death Row would soon fill it.

I walked over to Yard Side and climbed to the third tier. Once there, though, I faced quite a wait. The gate was, of course, locked, and the officer was a long way down the tier. He was the one I had to wait for; he was the one with the keys.

As I waited, my feelings weighed heavily. Gabriel had just been transferred, and although I accepted every official opinion about his history with sexual obsession, I still experienced what had occurred as some kind of defeat. Some part of me felt humanity had just suffered a blow and did not want to acknowledge that there are times that caring is most properly expressed by severing contact.

Before falling asleep the previous night, I'd seen an image of prison as a brick wall I kept hurling my body against. I knew my body would certainly be crushed long before even the slightest of dents appeared in the brick wall.

But I wasn't standing in a puncture-proof vest on the third tier of East Block in order to share my bad mood with Elmo. I prayed to "channel light," as folks in the rest of Marin County put it. The thought of that New Age sensibility surrounding San Quentin made me smile. So when the officer finally arrived, I was able to return his jokes and walk with a fairly easy step down to the cell where Elmo lay stretched on his bunk.

"Hey, what are you doing here?" Elmo rose and walked to the bars. "What's happening, what's up?"

I told him of my intention to visit while he was in the hole. Then I searched for a funny story in the midst of a week that included Gabriel's transfer and escalating fights between Ralph and Jan during *Godot* rehearsals.

"Monday night Genny Lim visited class. Remember her? The woman who put *Island* together? That book that compiled the poems that had been carved into cells on Angel Island by Chinese immigrants? Remember?"

Elmo nodded.

"This time she read her own poems, from her new book. There were lots about growing up in Chinatown and one that referred to her father's car, a LaSalle. Well, Rafael—you know, the older guy, new in our class?—got this wistful look on his face, and he sighed, 'Ah, a LaSalle!' He told us his first time at San Quentin was on account of a LaSalle. He was young, and he stole the car off the street and had it one week before he was picked up. He spent one year at San Quentin for that week with the LaSalle. Then, it was so funny, Elmo. Rafael paused in his story, smiled, and summed up, 'But, you know, it was worth it: That LaSalle was a *beautiful* car!'"

Elmo laughed, as I'd hoped that he would. Then he launched into his own story about LaSalles and his love for old cars and building low riders as a teenager, and we stood there in dank East Block, on either side of those bars, talking and laughing.

For weeks Ralph and Jan had been having small feuds. Ralph, who had spent so much time studying the play in the months before Jan arrived for rehearsals, often thought he knew better than the director.

Each morning as I walked into the prison, Spoon rose from his perch in the spiral staircase, walked over, and accompanied me to our office. He never mentioned the disagreements, but when Jim asked directly, Spoon shook his head and quoted the play, using that line one or another of us repeated almost daily: "That's how it is on this bitch of an earth."

After a blowup too big to pass over, Jan asked me to show up at the next day's rehearsal. Jan talked gently, trying to give Ralph a graceful way to continue as Gogo. But Ralph lashed out at everyone in the room, backing himself further and further into an impossible corner. J.B., the man who had replaced Gabriel as Lucky, tried to soothe Ralph, but to no avail.

A frustrated Jan finally spat out, "Stop being so childish!" To which Ralph replied, "I quit!"

Ralph gathered his large body, mustering all the dignity he could. His walk out of that room was Ralph's tour de force performance.

With barely four months until the first performance, Gogo was gone. Jan looked at the remainder of his cast, sighed deeply, and quoted the play: "Nothing to be done."

The very next day, Twin brought someone to read for Ralph's part. Happy was an old friend of Twin's; both men were from South Central. Although at first reading from a script was as unfamiliar to Happy as it had been to most of the others, the rapport between the two home boys was immediately apparent. In a very short time, Twin and Happy were incorporating high fives and moon walking into rehearsals, and work on *Godot* took off again.

The nature of my job at the prison during my first two and one-half years had allowed me to focus on my class, the men who were in it, and the poetry we shared. Thus, real human bonds had developed. For example, though Elmo and I had encountered difficult times, he had never written me off, nor had I ever stopped caring about him or admiring his intelligence and spirit. I was at San Quentin as a poet and teacher and was, therefore—even with the limitations prison protocol imposed—able to be on the side of my students. But by the time I watched Ralph walk away from that rehearsal in March 1988, my role at San Quentin had begun to change. By that spring, *Godot* was demanding Arts-in-Corrections' full and constant attention. I loved the play, was impressed with Jan's vision, and was pleased by the chance for Twin, Happy, Spoon, J.B., and Danny to challenge themselves and to prove to the world that they were more than mere "inmates." Without making a conscious decision, I had found myself doing whatever was required to help Jim and Denise pull off a successful *Godot*.

This "whatever" asked very little of me as a poet, teacher, or free spirit, and instead asked that I become some kind of administrative assistant. Each week, more and more journalists and theater folks wanted to visit rehearsals; each week our plans for the public performance enlarged; each week we had to complete a mountain of paperwork in order to gain prison permission for every aspect of the project. In order to be part of the team that would give

149

life to *Godot* at San Quentin, I had to be more attuned to the needs of the administration and staff. This shift from outsider to insider revealed aspects of myself that would occasionally shock and disturb me.

"Arts-in-Corrections requests permission . . . " Early on, Jim had taught me to compose the memos I would have to write and have signed in order to do almost anything at San Quentin. I wrote memos for classes I wanted to offer, memos for guest artists, memos to create and then distribute our anthologies, chapbooks, broadsides, audio- and videotapes. Carrying memos around from the captain's office to the chief deputy warden, to the warden himself sometimes occupied the bulk of a week.

Now *Godot* had quadrupled Arts-in-Corrections' output of memos. One day in June, I sat in the office and—just for fun—counted the memos Jim, Denise, and I had written to date regarding the play. Still one month away from performance, I counted more than fifty.

The first one was dated February 6, 1987, and requested permission to videotape our initial inmate reading. This memo bore four signatures in addition to Jim's: Luis's, the captain's, the chief deputy warden's, and the warden's. The most recent, dated June 6, 1988, listed clothing and props stored for the play in our new Art Center, where rehearsals were now held. There were one pair of beige pants with suspenders, five bowler hats, one pair of black lace-up men's shoes, one wood pipe (smoking), one gold watch, plus twenty-five additional items, including one wig (blond) and one buggy whip, which, each individually, had been the subject of more than one memo. (Lucky's rope still hadn't been approved, and I'd given up counting the hours Jim had already logged trying to get permission for that one. Final approval would be granted, contingent on Jim's storing the rope in a special locked box and signing it out each time it was used.)

At the bottom of the list were four "Items Not Yet Here But Will Be Part Of The Inventory When They Arrive: one bulb at-

omizer, one small tree, one large rock, one folding camp stool."
This memo had to be signed by Jim and nine folks higher up the
chain of command.

This is what Jim taught me: Write a narrative, outlining every-
thing you can think of—where and when the proposed event will
occur; which inmates, and how many, will be involved; how these
inmates will get to where they are supposed to be; how custody
will be provided; if people from the outside will come in, who will
meet them at the gate and escort them inside; the impact on bud-
get; what equipment will be involved, where this equipment will
be stored, and how it will be moved from one spot to another; what
the benefit of your request is to the institution.

"Anticipate every logistical and security concern and address it,"
Jim said, advising that I go to any staff likely to be involved *before*
writing the memo in order to find out what their needs were.
"Then," Jim warned, "make sure it all happens exactly as you
wrote that it would."

In addition to memos, we filled out security clearance forms for
anyone visiting inside San Quentin—guest artists, journalists, oc-
casional instructors, and so on. Prison staff then ran a security
check using the visitor's social security or driver's license number.
Once the visitor was cleared, we filled out a gate clearance form.
Without an approved gate clearance form, no one from outside
would be let in.

In the "cover your ass" world of a large institution, Jim taught
me to keep documentation for everything the poetry program had
ever done. Once a phone call came in to an associate warden in-
forming him that three prisoners had just won an animation prize
offered by the *Joan Rivers Show*. The associate warden stormed
into Jim's office. "This must be illegal," he fumed. Jim turned
around and pulled from the file cabinet the memo that had au-
thorized Tri-Con Productions—three men in an Arts-in-Correc-
tions' animation class—to submit their animation to the contest.

"I'll tell you," Jim later said, "I've never been so happy in my entire life to find a memo with the warden's signature right there in ink!"

But San Quentin was not only a huge bureaucracy requiring reams of paperwork, it was also a maximum security prison. So, for example, when Jim and I sat in Denise's office preparing the invitation we would send out to the public, in addition to the usual who, what, where, and when, we had to include a few prison "how-to's." We wrote:

> Certain special security measures must be taken to ensure your ability to enter and exit San Quentin at the conclusion of your evening in prison.
> Please Read the Following:
>
> Do Not wear blue.
> Do make sure to bring a current driver's license or State picture ID.
> Alcohol, drugs and weapons are prohibited on State Prison grounds.
> Vehicles are subject to search.
> Please arrive at San Quentin at 4:00 P.M. for institutional processing.

"Do you think we should make some comment, letting folks know we're aware, too, of how strange this all is?" I asked. "Maybe we can think of some clever phrase to put at the bottom."

Jim, Denise, and I looked at each other and said in unison, "That's how it is on this bitch of an earth." And Denise wrote the line at the end of the list of rules.

All of us Arts-in-Corrections artist/teachers—Lynnelle, Peter, Aida, Sara, and the rest—had mixed feelings about *Godot*. The play took up so much of Jim's time that our regular poetry, painting, drawing, music, and juggling programs suffered. We all loved *Godot*, especially Jan's visionary fervor and his work with the cast, but we debated among ourselves the value of putting so much time and effort into one spectacular project that actually involved very few prisoners, as opposed to ongoing programs that, though less glitzy, touched more of San Quentin's population. Though we didn't blame Jim—who was swept up by the wave of *Godot* and doing his best to steer the ship through rough waters—we were sometimes resentful. Jan and many of his visitors disregarded the rules and ignored San Quentin's small-town "perception is all" reality. Jim spent many hours covering for Jan and making sure the director's transgressions would not be fatal to *Godot* and, ultimately, to all of Arts-in-Corrections. We knew Jan would leave in July, and the rest of our programs would suffer whatever damage his flamboyance had caused.

I wondered if prison staff felt a similar resentment toward all of us Arts-in-Corrections artists. I remembered a story Elmo had told me of a theater workshop held long ago at San Quentin that he had covered for the *San Quentin News*. John Bergman and Geese Theater offered the workshop, but at first prisoners refused to participate. "You know," Elmo explained, "that macho thing. Everyone protecting his image."

However, the actors were not discouraged. Instead, they brought out a bagful of masks. With a mask to place over his face, each man began to join in.

"Bergman had the men jumping around like french fries," Elmo chuckled. "He had them being silly."

And then, Elmo said, less silly. In the course of that workshop, the visiting actors led the masked prisoners through a series: each man's first crime, being sentenced, walking in as a fish (a newcomer), the first night in a cell, visiting with his woman in the prison's visiting room.

"There was nothing the men wouldn't try with masks over their faces," Elmo remembered, still impressed.

I was impressed, too, and had asked Jim about the workshop. Jim spoke of one guard who looked in on the men in their masks. "How come these *artists*," he sneered at Jim, "come in for a couple of evenings, and inmates open right up? I work here day after day, bring them their mail, or whatever, and all I'm ever called is K9?"

The changes I noticed in myself went deeper than simply becoming a person who spent a great deal of time doing paperwork and thinking about security needs; these changes went beyond engaging in a rational debate about how Arts-in-Corrections could best be of use to prisoner-students and pondering whether guards were resentful because they had to play the heavy while artists got to have fun with prisoners. Rather, I noticed I myself was beginning to have little tolerance for that artistic intensity I'd valued my whole life.

For six months actors, photographers, film crews, critics, and drama students from both Sweden and the Bay Area had frequently visited rehearsals. Most of these visitors were very nice folks, and their interest in the prisoner cast and their work was an encouragement to the men as they worked on *Godot*. Many of these visitors even committed themselves for the duration—finding props, acting as stage manager, contacting critics, spreading the word—in ways that helped make our production successful.

However, the demands of some of these visitors and their tendency to break the rules and distort the truth made me furious. If some folks on the outside saw all prisoners as monsters, many of these guests—discovering that Twin, Happy, Spoon, J.B., and Danny were intelligent, articulate men, capable of great feeling—proclaimed the cast paragons of brilliance and courage. I didn't fault the prisoners for enjoying and taking advantage of this adulation. (Before rehearsal one day, Jim and I began moving props. Jim asked for help and Twin said, "I don't have to; I'm a star.") I thought it sad, though, that people locked up couldn't simply be recognized as human beings, but must be either beasts or heroes.

Because many of our *Godot* visitors dealt only with Jim, Denise, or me, we became the face of the "system" to them; we were the ones keeping them from what they saw as their rights as free agents. Seeing myself in the role of authority and protector of the institution for the first time in my life came as quite a shock. And discovering that, in fact, I *did* feel more allegiance to San Quentin than to these visitors who had no stake in the ongoing work of Arts-in-Corrections astounded me. I wondered if "long-term, in-depth" inevitably meant becoming part of the institution where one worked. And if so, would becoming an insider destroy the heart of what I was at San Quentin to do?

I'd first asked myself a similar question soon after I had begun teaching cell to cell. In all lockup units, there was that locked gate between the staircase and each tier of cells. When I would come to the unit to work with men on their poems, I would have to wait for an officer to walk by with the keys to unlock this gate. If the officer was taking a prisoner to the showers or rolling the food cart down the tier, I might have to wait a long while.

One day I climbed the metal staircase as usual, then stood on the top step patiently. The officer came down the tier laughing. He pointed to the gate, and I saw that it was ajar. He said, "It sure didn't take you long to become institutionalized!"

In my first weeks at the prison, I walked as my students told me they must always walk: with all my senses alert. I walked as though I were in some foreign country, hungry for each new sensory clue. I noticed each rattling of a keychain, each shout of "Escort!," each new man in an orange jumpsuit being led handcuffed onto the grounds. I listened to familiar words—kite, juice, fish, car, beef, jacket—used in unfamiliar contexts. Since I didn't yet understand the meaning of what my eyes noticed or what my ears heard, I gave each event my full attention. It took barely more than a year, how-ever, for me to so much expect the gate before me to be locked that I didn't even look. And now, nearly two years later, it seemed I felt closer to someone like Associate Warden Tabash, a thirty-year prison employee, than to artists with revolutionary sensibilities.

The event that shone the brightest light on this realization con-cerned a young Swedish woman who had received the prison's per-mission to attend rehearsals and make sketches that would even-tually be exhibited in Stockholm. Each day Lotta accompanied Jan into the prison. She sat through rehearsals drawing, and over time, she and Spoon fell in love.

Because Lotta and Spoon came together under Arts-in-Corrections' auspices, their love was a blatant transgression of the prison's rule about overfamiliarity, and, therefore, put the arts program in danger. Because of this, Jim told Lotta she could no longer come into the prison as an artist sponsored by Arts-in-Corrections. Spoon and Lotta felt that we—Jim, Denise, and I—were opposed to their love, which wasn't true. Whatever doubts we had resulted from the fact that Lotta treated the three of us with so much disdain, as though we were the enemy standing in the way of true love. Her enmity caused us to wonder if Lotta was good enough for Spoon, of whom we were all very fond.

Spoon and Lotta had tried to keep their love private, not wanting to disrupt the course of the play; they planned to get married once performances were over. But when their love was discovered and Lotta was told she could no longer come to rehearsals, they moved up the plans for their wedding. Because of the heat coming down on Arts-in-Corrections, Jim wasn't going to attend the ceremony. He said it was my call, but I'd make his life easier if I didn't attend, either. Though Spoon had been rude to us all for weeks, my feelings for him hadn't changed, so my loyalty to Jim pulled me one way and my caring for Spoon another.

Ultimately, I took the easy way out and let events make my decision. On the day of the wedding, a film crew from New York put me through hoop after hoop. After a morning of trying to meet their demands, I looked up to see Pat at the door to our office informing us Spoon and Lotta were now married.

The words Elmo used as epigraph in his chapbook were Martin Luther King, Jr.'s: "The ultimate measure of a man is not where he stands in moments of comfort and convenience, but where he stands at times of challenge and controversy." *Godot* had wrung me out, but by not attending Spoon's wedding, I knew in some very deep way I'd just measured short.

Spoon, brother of my soul, stopped talking to me. After days of silence, I walked by him as he sat in that spiral staircase and heard his voice as I passed: "Give me back your copies of my poems."

I turned and spoke, hurt and angry. "Do you mean that? After all these years, do you mean that?"

I insisted we talk, and in my own transgression of paragraph 3400, Spoon and I walked into a closed studio at SQTV and sat down. At first, we both were well covered with defensive armor, but it didn't take long before we were in tears. We poured out our feelings and rose from that talk able to be close once again.

During the last weeks before performance, Jim's workday was often from eight in the morning until ten at night, so when a prisoner at the door to the office asked, "Can I get you to sign this tomorrow? Will you be here?" Jim, exhausted, responded, "I live here."

The prisoner paused, caught Jim's eye, and reminded him of the truth: "*I* live here," he said.

This man and the others locked behind San Quentin's bars did indeed live here. And despite the heightened air surrounding *Godot*, despite Jan's dramatic fervor, despite all the talk of the play as a "primal scream," Jan's description was accurate: The play *was* like the diary of these three thousand men. As Twin put it:

> Each day you live in prison, you're waiting for something. You're waiting for a phone call you may never get, for a letter you may never get, for a release date that may never come if you've got life tops, which each one of us has. So it's not really acting to me; it touches bases with a lot of things as far as prison life is concerned. It's confinement—two alone with nowhere to go, nothing to do, and you're open for something. That's what I get out of it, because it fits and touches with what I'm going through day by day.

Although my days continued to be filled with demands unrelated to my own work as artist-in-residence, I loved the play, and whenever I could I dropped by the Art Center to watch Twin, Happy,

Spoon, J.B., and Danny work with Jan. I was filled with awe and deep joy as I listened to the cast speak Beckett's lines. I loved watching Twin speak in the second act after Pozzo and Lucky have fallen and Didi and Gogo debate helping them up. "It's not every day that we are needed," Vladimir began. "Not indeed that we personally are needed. Others would meet the case equally well, if not better. To all mankind they were addressed, those cries still ringing in our ears! But at this place, at this moment of time, all mankind is us, whether we like it or not. Let us make the most of it, before it is too late! Let us represent worthily for once the foul brood to which a cruel fate consigned us!"

"To all mankind they were addressed, those cries still ringing in our ears!" I might dislike Jan's personal theatrics and get angry with visiting artists and film crews, but watching the men rehearse reminded me that we were all in this together. Jan, the cast, the visiting artists, Jim, Denise, prison administration, staff, and I were all involved in the task of trying to make this fantastic thing happen, this play in prison. And, more fundamentally, we were all in this *life* together, human beings doing our best. Watching the men rehearse brought me back, as art should, to the knowledge that "at this place, at this moment of time, all mankind is us, whether we like it or not."

Jan noted that prisoners know what silence is about. He spoke of watching men in cell blocks stand at the bars, listening to the silence: "That's a language they really understand." Under Jan's direction, half the play was silence, and he instructed his cast very specifically, move by move, choreographing speech, silence, and gesture with an eye to the shapes made onstage by the men in relation to each other.

I loved watching Spoon, who certainly knew about silence, work his way toward Pozzo's roaring. As Pozzo, Spoon ranted, "Have you not done tormenting me with your accursed time?" Then he continued more calmly, "They give birth astride of a grave, the light gleams an instant, then it's night once more."

On many days, when I dropped by at the Art Center, Chris was there, too. "Way to go, Chris," I thought to myself. It would have been so easy for Chris to have responded to Ralph's dramatic exit from *Godot* with some version of "I told you so." Instead, Chris watched the rehearsals with curiosity and interest and led the applause during the performance held for main-line inmates.

One of the responsibilities I'd taken on was gathering the text for the playbill, and one afternoon I went to the Art Center with this task in mind. I sat down with each actor and asked for what he most wanted to say about his work on this play.

Twin said, "I feel a big connection to Vladimir and his situation because, look where I'm at. Here you wait for a visit, you wait for a letter. You wait for the courts. It's just like waiting for Godot. . . .

"There we are, on this road, this mountaintop, wherever it's at. We're waiting on something and it's never happening, and we're just having our own little frustrations, or there are arguments. Our little happiness."

Happy said, "The characters within this play are a reflection of me and the position I'm in. The pain and suffering Estragon goes through and feels for his friend is like my pain and suffering. Estragon is tired of waiting for something that isn't coming. I feel that way, too."

Spoon spoke of how the play's truth was apparent on a daily basis and added, "This truth is universal: tragedy and humor existing within the same moment, love and hate sharing the same space. . . . As human beings, we all have one foot in light and one foot in darkness."

J.B. said, "*Godot* says something about the hopelessness of life, the horror of realizing you're an individual, and there's actually no one in the universe remotely like you, and no certainty about who you are or what your true purpose is. It's about life, confronting the possibility of faith (is there anything worth waiting for?)."

And Danny said of his role as the Boy, who closes each act with a message from Godot that "he won't come this evening, but surely tomorrow": "Being a spiritual person, it seems I'm bringing a message from God to keep our faith, to hang on through it all. This is my own message from God to myself, so I, too, carry this message to all of us."

....

Close to six hundred people attended the three evening performances for the public. These folks included F. Murray Abraham (Lincoln Center's Pozzo), Bill Irwin, CDC director James Rowland, and my Sara. One must be eighteen to visit inside San Quentin, and Sara had turned eighteen five days before opening night. This was her first glimpse of the world that had enveloped her mother for nearly three years. J.B.'s wife attended, as did Danny's mother and Spoon's wife and brother. Twin's and Happy's mothers and sisters came up from LA.

Each night, close to two hundred people lined up outside the prison's gates to begin a long process of entry. When a person reached the head of the line, Denise or I would check his or her name against our lists of those who had passed security clearance. Next, the person walked through a metal detector and moved on to a gathering hall, where Sergeant Egan informed the whole group of the prison's no-hostage policy: If a free person was taken hostage, the prison would negotiate for his or her release, but would not trade an inmate's freedom for that of the hostage. Although the purpose behind this policy was to reduce the likelihood of hostage taking, the warning sounded ominous, and reminded visitors that they were indeed entering prison.

Before the first night's performance, F. Murray Abraham introduced himself to San Quentin's Pozzo and asked, "About the blind thing, how did you work on that?"

Spoon said, "I closed my eyes, to tell you the truth."

"I wear a blindfold," Abraham responded, nodding approval. "It's the only way to get the real feeling."

....

Jim and Jan had created a makeshift stage at one end of the gym. A black drop cloth on the flat floor delineated the stage. A guard with a rifle patrolled on the gun rail above us, and each performance was punctuated with the ringing of a phone during institutional count. The audience sat on hard bleachers, pushed underneath the gym's balcony in order to maintain the gun officer's view of the floor, and put up with horrid acoustics. This was the theater in which San Quentin's *Godot* had to play.

Each night, however, a hush fell on the house as Twin spoke the long speech that began, "Was I sleeping while the others suffered? Am I sleeping now?" At the beginning of the second act, Twin turned Vladimir's song into a soulful blues. When Twin pulled out his shades, put them on, and began singing in falsetto "Then all the dogs came running," the audience nearly went wild.

During every performance, I got the chills when Gogo, standing on that black drop cloth over San Quentin's gym floor, below that patrolling guard on the gun rail, asked, "We've lost our rights?" and Didi responded, staring out into vast space, "We got rid of them."

The last performance ended, as had the previous ones, with Finney—an inmate in his prison blues—playing the flute. Although there could be no total blackout, Jim had received permission to dim the lights at the show's opening and close. And in that brief, muted darkness, *Godot* at San Quentin ended.

After that last performance, Happy's mother told a reporter that the play seemed to be saying that God doesn't answer, no one appears to answer, but we keep waiting anyway. She said that when she heard Finney's flute, she felt that her son was personally crying out for help. She said she could hear her son saying, "I'm not bad; I'm human, too."

"There was so much emotion, no pretense," Happy's mother concluded. "As a mother, it hurts."

Sergeant Egan told the milling crowds it was time to go home. Twin, Happy, Spoon, J.B., and Danny were hailed by an enthusiastic audience, then strip-searched before being led back to their cells.

nine

"Which Side Are You On?"

In the weeks following *Godot*, I often thought of a comment made by the journalist Lawrence Weschler on the second night of performance. Ren said that if he was going to cover the story, this is where he would begin: After the admiring audience had gone home, after the theater had been turned back into a gym, after the last of the reviews had been read, after the stars were once again known by their prison ID numbers.

As the audience milled with the cast after the last San Quentin performance, Bill had kindly warned J.B., "For any actor, this will be the hard time. Now, after the play's closed."

"Bittersweet," J.B. had responded, nodding.

"Bittersweet," Bill Irwin agreed.

....

By the summer of 1988, I had been teaching at San Quentin for three years. Even during the first year of once-a-week classes, when my experience was limited to what I shared with my students in our classroom, to Jim's advice as he walked me inside, and to the few remarks I overheard staff speak at Four Post—I saw San Quentin as a world constructed by shifting points of view. My nature and interests caused me to notice the "this, and also that" character of prison, and what I noticed led me to begin writing the first of my poems in the voices of others. My perception of "the Truth" as composed of each individual small truth placed side by side made me desire to see the "whole of which I was given only part."

My desire to see committed me to honor each of what appeared to be opposing positions. But my work on *Godot*—demanding, as it did, that I look at San Quentin through the eyes of its administration—had made me understand that it was only as an outsider that I could choose to perceive these oppositions as merely apparent. For most everyone else at the prison, these oppositions were not apparent, but real: convict and cop, administration and custody staff, free people and custody, black prisoners and white prisoners, and on and on. As artist-in-residence, I had the luxury of cutting across the grain of prison's adversarial reality and looking for what everyone shared: being human.

"They say in Harlan County/There are no neutrals there," began one verse of the song I so loved. "You'll either be a union man/Or a thug for J.H. Blair./Which side are you on?/Which side are you on?" At San Quentin, I wondered if it was possible not to choose sides without being neutral? Was it possible to be passionate, not about one side or the other, but about wholeness? I knew that in order to sustain such a vision, I had to continue to strengthen my ability to live with paradox.

The grant gave me time for this strengthening, and time brought me the support and challenge required to grow stronger. Elmo was the guide without whom I would never have been able to make the journey, and he was also the externalized voice of my own inner critic. Spoon's silence and speech were both solace. Responding to Gabriel's love hurt my heart, distressed my mind, *and* sharpened my vision.

When I'd rush ahead in my breathless manner, one of my students surely would say, "Relax, we're not going anywhere." And, for those years, neither was I. Whether we shared the pleasure of guest artists and creating chapbooks, or those "warts and all" revelations of disappointment and anger, each Monday night, there we were—together, learning more about each other, growing closer.

As I spent more and more hours each week at the prison, what my senses encountered expanded from the closed world of our classroom and Four Post to the call of gulls sounding through West Block; men and women in green running full speed to answer an alarm whistle; catcalls from the weight pile; the shadows barbed wire casts; Suzan walking through East Block in a dress and high heels; B.B. King playing "The Thrill Is Gone" to an audience of convicts out on the yard; Lynnelle's desk covered with slides of work by her Death Row students; Henry responding to a prisoner's request for a favor with "I don't do favors for inmates; now, what do you need?"; a teaching artist telling me at an Arts-in-Corrections conference about the dance her macho male prison students had just choreographed; the roar of the print shop as I delivered copy for *Godot*'s playbill; Jonesy in "officer green" joining Aida's inmate band on the keyboard; the warden with his hand on the phone as I sat at the massive table at the center of his office; handing the Arts-in-Corrections class list to Officer Weichel at his desk on the Porch; an officer leading a handcuffed man across the Upper Yard, the two men talking about the World Series; Spoon in that spiral staircase; the sound of guns being fired at the rifle range; handing my car key to the officer at East Gate and watching him open the trunk to make sure there was no escaping prisoner curled up inside, before he placed the key back in my palm, opened the gate, and waved me homeward.

Now the Arts-in-Corrections manager, Bill Cleveland, hired me to create a book-length manual for artists teaching in prison, and I was asked to expand my vision still wider. Bill wanted chapters on the history of Arts-in-Corrections, on rules and vocabulary, and such. He wanted lists of prisons and artist/facilitators' phone numbers, but he wanted the bulk of the book to be a novella in which each chapter was told from the point of view of a different person at a hypothetical prison: a guest artist visiting for the first time, an artist/facilitator, an associate warden, a maximum security prisoner, a teaching artist, a community resources manager, a minimum security prisoner on his way home, an officer, and the spouse of the teaching artist.

Bill thought, as I did, that the best way to convey the reality of prison to one coming in to work as an artist was to present the viewpoints, desires, and needs of a wide range of involved people. In preparation for writing, I began to travel around the state interviewing prisoners, wardens, teaching artists, and others. In the following months I would experience "this, and also that" to the max.

Another Wednesday afternoon in East Block. Elmo had told me he was to have a major hearing that morning, and as soon as I saw his face, I knew the results had not been good. We talked for a while, but the main thing on Elmo's mind was getting the news to his wife. He asked if I'd make a phone call to her.

I grimaced and sighed: for me to make such a call would be a major prison transgression. Yet here was Elmo, unable to get crucial news to the woman he loved. *I* had the privilege of looking from a wide angle, but Elmo was locked in this cell, and his point of view was focused and specific.

"Elmo, I can't," I said.

"Not *can't*, Judith. Won't."

From where he stood on his side of the cell bars, Elmo was right. Once, before learning the full import of the prohibition against such an act, I'd even made such a phone call for him. I knew that San Quentin would suffer no dangerous security breach if I called Elmo's wife to tell her the result of the morning's hearing; I knew that Elmo, here in lockup, had no access to legitimate phone calls; I knew his wife must be waiting in worry.

With my *Godot* experience behind me, I also knew that from the point of view of the administration, making that phone call would be a serious breach of paragraph 3400. One Arts-in-Corrections teaching artist had stepped out of similar bounds, and although everyone knew that this man had acted from the very best of heartfelt intentions, his deed had caused prison officials to so question his judgment that they asked him to leave San Quentin forever.

Though I wanted the luxury of seeking the whole in which Elmo's need and the prison's rule were each only part, San Quentin demanded action rather than vision. "Which side are you on? Which side are you on?" Most days at the prison I was confronted with at least one situation—like this one with Elmo—in which, despite my sense that no matter which way I chose, I'd be wrong, I still had to choose. On that Wednesday, I refused to make the phone call, then walked down the tier with a heart full of sadness. My heartfelt emotion, though, did Elmo little good at that moment.

Later that year I heard the classicist and philosopher Martha Nussbaum on Bill Moyers's television show *A World of Ideas*. She said: "Often when you care deeply about more than one thing, the very course of life will bring you round to a situation where you can't honor both of the commitments. It looks like anything you do will be wrong, perhaps even terrible in some way." I turned up the television's volume. *Godot* might be the prisoner's San Quentin diary, as Jan put it, but these words were mine.

Nussbaum talked about the king's choice in Aeschylus's play *Agamemnon*. As a king trying to lead his army to Troy, Agamemnon encountered no wind to move the ships. The gods told him the only way to save his troops was to sacrifice his daughter. Nussbaum described Agamemnon's situation: "Two deep and entirely legitimate commitments coming into a terrible conflict in which there's not anything the king can do that will be without wrong doing."

Although most decisions I had to make at the prison *did* involve a conflict between human concern and ethical duty, I was well aware that my choices hardly bore the weight of Agamemnon's. Without forgetting Luis's warning that no matter how careful and cautious I might be, just my presence at San Quentin could lead to a fight on the yard, I recognized that the daily choices I had to make were unlikely to result in anyone's death.

All around me, however, were those who bore this exact burden. That unwritten but well-communicated "convict code" defined a system by which prisoner transgressions should be handled. Although I certainly was not privy to the inner workings of this code, I could see that my students' lives demanded adherence to a precise system of saving face and "handling business" that required each man pay vigilant attention to the choices he made.

Correctional officers and administrators operating within their own exact system were forced to make judgment calls all day long, knowing that, often, life or death hung in the balance. Among both convicts and cops, there were individuals who acted with little concern for any harm they may have caused and others who were willing to bear the burden of their choices. There were incidents in which prisoners covered up for their fellow convicts and incidents in which staff lied to protect their brothers-in-arms. But in spite of the convict code and prison protocol, there were individuals— both prisoners and staff—who instinctively made judgment calls as actual responses, as attempts to make the best choice at the moment, given the available information.

I was in awe of these folks' abilities to accept the prisoner-guard game, process an enormous amount of conflicting information quickly, act as well as they were able, and live with the consequences if what they saw as their best choice turned out to be a poor choice indeed.

For none of these capacities was mine. "Just spit it out" was the most common reply to my stuttered attempts to express the complexity I observed in most situations. When, having to act, I made decisions Elmo disagreed with, he accused me of spending too much time with staff and choosing duty over heart. Some days he was right.

Some days were even worse than that. Some days I felt burnt out. On those days, everyone at San Quentin, including me, seemed stuck in a world in which manipulation was the only way to get one's needs met. On such days, whoever I encountered seemed to be using me for his or her own purpose, and I felt resentful, tired, and desirous only of taking the easiest exit.

Some days were better, and I perceived the world as Jim most often viewed it: as a world in which each choice was not an either/or, but an opportunity for a win/win. Jim looked for the approach that would give staff, prisoners, and the arts program what each most wanted and needed. Some days I was able to shift my sight to see the win/win lurking within an apparently either/or choice. If that Wednesday in East Block had been such a day, I might have been able to find a way to get the news to Elmo's wife without breaking prison rules.

Best of all were the rare moments when I was given that vision I prayed for, and I was able to *be* so fully that my actions expressed wholeness.

....

One day in mid-July, as I made my rounds collecting signatures on the memo requesting permission for our next class project, I noticed a stapled blue pamphlet on the desk of each office I entered. I glanced at the title, *Crime and Punishment in the Year 2000: What Kind of Future?*, and asked to look at a copy. It contained a summary of the proceedings of a forum sponsored by the National Council on Crime and Delinquency (NCCD). An attached San Quentin routing slip asked recipients for comment. The anonymous quote that was used as the pamphlet's epigraph read: "If we don't change our direction, we are going to end up where we are headed."

Huh? Here at San Quentin, this world of judgment calls and instant street slickness, folks were being asked to pause and consider?

Intrigued, I kept reading: "The criminal justice system is simply ill-equipped to have a major impact on reducing crime in the future. Instead, we must recommit ourselves as a nation to improving the quality of life for all Americans through means other than the criminal justice system."

Had Berkeley radicals infiltrated the prison and put this literature on the desk of every man and woman of rank at San Quentin? I flipped the pages to see just who'd been at this NCCD-sponsored conference and found, yes, there were a couple professors, but mostly there were probation and parole officers, policemen, directors of state departments of corrections and juvenile systems, folks from the Federal Bureau of Prisons, and representatives from state offices of the attorney general. No, not Berkeley radicals.

I ran (not literally—it was against every rule to run, for running connoted major-league crisis—I *walked* very quickly) to the offices of particular staff, sat myself down, opened the blue pamphlet, and said, "Listen to this."

I read statistics about the increasing gap between the "haves" and "have nots," about the need for job training, education, drug prevention and health care, and private industry to remain in inner cities. "Only when we begin to successfully address these root causes of crime," I read out loud, "will the need for the criminal justice and correctional enterprise begin to diminish, which is our ultimate aim."

As I read, I noticed my hand-picked audience of sergeants, lieutenants, and associate wardens nodding their heads. What was happening? These men and women who most often made ballot-box decisions opposite my own agreed: "If we simply attempt to solve the crime problem by more severe forms of punishment, we'll fail to achieve the primary goal of creating a far more healthy society."

For a few days, I was dumbfounded. Then I began to approach conversations with staff differently. Instead of asking "what would you do if . . . ," I asked people to describe the world that they saw.

This line of conversation—the one that described children and parents and institutions and hope and discouragement—allowed us to focus on the feelings we shared instead of the opinions, judgment calls, and political rhetoric that divided us.

Walking away from these conversations, I wondered once again what it might be like to inhabit a world where there was time to discover agreement in what at first looked like dissension. I wondered what currently unimagined actions might emerge from such a commitment to wholeness.

I had participated in one community experience born of such a commitment. In Point Arena in the late 1970s, the school board was in the process of hiring a new principal, and parents were divided. Old-timers wanted someone who would honor the 3 Rs, back-to-the-land folks wanted someone committed to openness and innovation, and a group from the Baptist church wanted someone who would uphold the values it cherished.

The school board responded to weeks' worth of raucous meetings by opening a room at the school for six hours a day one weekend, and parents dropped by when they could. The point of these weekend meetings was not to come up with a solution—the job description the board would use to conduct its candidate search—but to allow people to tell their own stories.

I sat in that room for hour after hour listening to people I thought of as different from me. When we had talked to each other at the level of pedagogical ideas and theories, we had always disagreed. But during those two days of open meetings, I heard how all of us loved our children, how we felt school had not served us as well as we would have liked when we were young and was not serving our children well now, how we all had fears. In our own ways, we each wanted to raise children who would grow into adults capable of making a decent life for themselves and contributing to the lives of others. Any slight move toward asking "what should we do?" led to disagreement, but when we hung out next to the bones of our stories, we felt very close.

Of course, once the weekend was over, the school board still had to take action and find a new principal. But the two days without action beyond speaking and listening well had strengthened the capacity of each of us to be part of a community with others we saw as different from ourselves.

....

Most of my San Quentin students agreed that *tolerating* points of view other than one's own was necessary, but they remained resistant to my own excitement about actually using my lips to *express* the words of another. Earlier that winter, when *Godot* was first in rehearsal, I'd asked the poet Joan Swift to come in as a guest artist. Joan had been raped many years before. The man who raped her had been found and put in prison. After his release, he raped—and murdered—another woman. Joan was a witness in the sentencing phase of the trial for this latter offense. Afterward, she wrote a sequence of poems, "Testimony," in which each poem assumed the voice of a different person at that trial. There were poems in the voice of the victim, her husband, the prosecuting attorney, the criminal's mother, his sister, and Joan herself. Joan's poems, unlike my own, were not poems of imagination. Hers incorporated actual words spoken by real people.

I liked Joan's poems very much and thought my students would, too. And since CDC Director Rowland emphasized victims' needs and concerns, we had received enthusiastic permission to do a taped reading and interview with Joan at SQTV before class. I thought I'd scored a win/win. Hardly.

In class, no matter how much Joan and I talked about the format of her poems, some of my students would not believe that the lines "The executioner always wears a hood. The ax gleams./ Blood spurts where his testicles slice off./Behind the eyeslits it is always me" were written in the voice of the murdered woman's husband and were not Joan's personal feelings. Chris argued that anyone able to write such lines must believe them. But Joan said, no, actually she herself was completely opposed to capital punishment. She read her poem "The Line-Up," which, she told us, expressed what she herself felt: "Each prisoner is so sad in the glare/I want to be his mother/ . . . O I would tell each one/he will wake small again/in some utterly new place!/Trees without bars sun a sweet juice/a green field full of pardon." But Chris shook his head, wouldn't listen to more, and left class early to return to his cell.

Elmo—who hadn't yet been sent to East Block—had no problem accepting the difference between Joan's personal perspective and the point of view of another, but he said the poems sounded so detached and literary. Elmo wanted to know how Joan felt, what the experience of rape had been for her.

Joan responded that after she'd been raped, the poems she wrote had been about her feelings. She read lines: " . . . your hulk/in through the door and my neck/seized like an ancient town./My throat full of its scream . . . " and " . . . But those two fierce hands/ of yours, they stay like islands/still unmapped, the palm's fate/ curving along my face." These were lines Elmo admired, the lines that did what he wanted poetry to do.

The next day, Spoon asked me to send Joan a copy of his chapbook. She sent a poem in return:

> **Spoon**
> *you choose stairs for listening*
> *outside the classroom at San Quentin,*
>
> *your black face solemn with wanting*
> *to hear some way out to the poem.*
>
> *Spoon, all of us down in the rock*
> *together, original walls*
>
> *too old now for leaving,*
> *you cross your legs in prison denim.*
>
> *Spoon, what crime do you hold in your*
> *hands, folding and folding?*

And why do I lure you close to others,
this once all week you can be alone?

Here are your words: keys, bars,
noise, constant yelling. *You*

wrote them. Here are the others:
woman, picnic, meadow. *Spoon,*

she wears grass like a scarf and carries
a basket. She leans to you from the top

step, up where the guard lets her past,
guns racked, cannas in the garden

bright with moon. Her muslin skirt
lightly touches your silence where she

passes around you, into you, through you,
doing her own sad time.

....

"I know, I know. This is *my* obsession," I said in late July as I described the next class project I had in mind: a sequence of poems—one poem by each student—in the voices of men out on the yard.

"This point-of-view nonsense *is* your obsession, true enough," Chris agreed. "But something about this here particular project sounds like ulterior motive."

Of course, Chris was right. I could always count on Chris—or Elmo, though he was in the hole and so not part of this conversation—to sniff out any whiff of what I might *not* be saying.

What I was saying was certainly true: I had more than established my interest in multiple points of view. Almost every one of my students had figuratively raised his hands and cried, "Enough already, enough!" In varying degrees, most of these men had let me know that for them, voice meant one's *own* voice, the voice of the poet. We'd been over this same ground so many times, beginning with my poems and most recently with those of Joan Swift; there had to be some reason, Chris Brown discerned, why I was coming at them again with my same drag.

I came at them this time because Bill Cleveland had hired Gary Glassman to create a public service video in conjunction with Arts-in-Corrections artists at various prisons, and Gary wanted my class to be part of the project. Rowland may have stopped using the word "rehabilitation," but returning prisoners to the larger community as useful, rather than destructive, citizens certainly seemed to be his intention. Rowland seemed to feel that such a return required restoration. Not only restoration *to* the prisoner of socially productive qualities and skills, but restoration *by* him or her. This latter required recognizing both the harm caused to one's victim, and the understanding that crime not only was committed against an individual but was a rupture of the community as a whole. Serving time might be part of the debt to be paid, but Rowland seemed interested in a more active giving back, an actual return.

Bill wanted to show Rowland how Arts-in-Corrections could contribute to this process. Prison artists could create murals for school walls, prison writers could create true-life public service announcements about the dangers of drugs, and so on. Thus Bill hired Gary, and I set myself up for Chris's well-developed ulterior-motive detection abilities.

In some sense, I was using my students both to further Bill's agenda and to explore one of my own. I believed it would be harder to cause harm to another person if one could see the world through his or her eyes. Perhaps writing poems in the voice of someone quite different from oneself might contribute to this process.

It seemed our involvement in this video project would give Rowland an example of prisoners giving back to the community, give Bill a chance to show Rowland Arts-in-Corrections' value, give me a chance to explore my hypothesis, and give my students a chance to be part of creating a project with Gary. Once again I thought I had a win/win/win/win situation; once again, Chris showed me I hadn't a clue.

Although the men—primarily out of kindness to me—put some half-hearted effort into this project, it made little sense to most of them to try to look at the world through the eyes of someone else. The day Gary arrived, he and I met with my students during afternoon outcount. Gary had been hired to create a product for a particular purpose, not to take the time necessary to explore with the San Quentin poets the best way to present their work. So although all my students liked Gary, most felt manipulated by Arts-in-Corrections. Only Carl, always supportive and polite, put sincere effort into rehearsing the piece he'd composed.

Carl was by far the oldest of my current students, and the only one who'd lived most of his life on the outside. The sentence he was serving was a relatively short one, and we all knew Carl was soon due to be released.

In midsummer 1988, Carl was one of only two white men in our class. He had been born in the Blue Ridge Mountains and he wrote in his chapbook, *In the Hills and Hollers:* "The hills. Now I tell you folks, we lived so fur back in the hills that it took a week for the radio waves to come in. Then, if you wus lucky, the waves would sorta fall into the holler and you could hear the Grand Ole Opry. The holler wus so deep you could see only two birds flying at a time.

"Take the railroad. No need, it is already gone. But when it wus there, it wus so crooked, the engineer could almost touch the cowbuse."

So here we had a slow-as-molasses, white, southern, old country boy in a room otherwise filled with quick-moving African American youngsters. An interesting setup.

But Carl was one of the most sincere human beings I've met in my whole life. His sweetness and straightforward Christian compassion warmed everyone's heart, even—maybe especially—Chris Brown's.

That afternoon, when count cleared, the men left for chow and Gary and I headed out to the snack bar. On our way back across the Plaza before 6:20 movement and the evening of videotaping we had planned, Carl's friend Leo rushed up to us. "Carl's in R&R," Leo told us.

R&R, Receiving and Release. This meant Carl was on his way home.

Gary and I walked around to R&R, and instead of the "Old Man," as some of the guys affectionately called Carl, we saw a lean, rangy dude with a twinkle in his eye. I was so happy for Carl, I could barely contain myself. Since nearly all my students were serving some kind of life sentence, this was the first time in three years I'd actually witnessed a man from my class as he was on his way out of San Quentin, and I treasured the moment.

As Gary and I turned to walk back to the Art Center and the filming ahead, Carl, true to form, apologized to us for cutting out before taping his poem. But even kind Carl didn't look *too* glum or contrite!

....

As part of the preparation for the point-of-view project with Gary, I'd given the men poems by the poet Frank Bidart. He wrote many poems in the voices of others—an anorexic woman in "Ellen West," the ballet dancer Vaslav Nijinsky in another long piece. I wanted my students to see how Bidart's poems spoke in the voice of another, how they incorporated a wide range of material—from historical texts to doctors' reports—and the way they appeared on the page. Bidart used punctuation, line and stanza break, and upper case letters to create a score that captured, as precisely as possible, an exact sound.

Bidart lived in Cambridge, but I had read that he would be giving a reading in August at the UC Berkeley campus, and I wrote to ask if he would be willing to visit my class. I also asked if the poet would come talk with Elmo, my primary point-of-view debate partner. Such a visit from an outsider to a lockup unit would be most unusual, of course, but I asked for, and received, special permission. Bidart accepted both invitations, but when the day of his visit rolled around, main line was locked down, so there was no class, and we walked straight toward East Block.

As Bidart and I walked down the long tier to Elmo's cell—both of us decked out in those camouflage-green vests—we were surrounded by the sound of a baseball game blaring from what seemed like every TV in the block. For the next hour or so, Elmo and Bidart stood on either side of the bars talking of poems while noise filled the cavern around them: "Strike three!" then "He's out!" followed by both raucous cheering and booing.

I watched the two men search for some body equivalent of the handshake that the bars and heavy screening rendered impossible. This was the moment I most often placed my open palm on the screening as a gesture of touch through so much layered steel. But Elmo and Bidart, who were after all strangers, instead leaned toward each other very slightly in greeting.

Elmo seemed to recognize that he was the host, and he welcomed Bidart to East Block with the dignity of a man receiving a guest in his home, though it happened to be humble. My heart filled watching Elmo's ability to be precisely who he was, precisely where he was, without either apology or self-righteousness. I was equally moved by Bidart, this gentle-seeming man standing within East Block's prison-at-its-roughest essence. I had no idea, of course, what his mind was noting or his body registering, but to all appearances Bidart was calm, meeting Elmo as a man and a poet. The two began to discuss the process of transcribing what one hears in one's head to the page, and I backed away to give them some degree of privacy.

The same steadiness I now observed in Bidart had impressed me at his reading in Berkeley earlier that week. There, too, the man had stood against gray concrete, for UC Berkeley's Architecture Building nearly matched East Block for cold, stark presence.

In Berkeley, Bidart had talked between poems about what it was to grow up in the Bakersfield, California, of the late '40s and ear-

ıs a boy who knew himself as gay, a boy who loved opera and refinement. Bidart was talking of difference, of sensing oneself as an Other, but that Berkeley audience kept encouraging Bidart to take easy jabs at Bakersfield's lack of cool.

That audience laughed, praising itself, as I grew angrier and angrier at what, to me, seemed arrogant privilege. Bidart resisted irony. He did not deny the difficulty of growing up different, but he refused to pander to the crowd.

Here in East Block, I watched a similar honesty. Although grunts and whoops surrounded Elmo and Bidart as they talked of poetry and the writing of poems, nothing in Bidart's stance indicated disdain for the men all around us. He just quietly—with beauty and attention—continued to talk to Elmo.

Suddenly a huge roar enveloped East Block, and when it died down, Bidart asked what it was like to write in the midst of such noise. Elmo spoke of staying up half the night to write and to read during the hours the block was nearly still. Bidart said he, too, often needed to withdraw from the world, to disconnect his phone, to stay inside solitude, in order to write.

Elmo passed his copy of Bidart's poem "The War of Vaslav Nijinsky" through the open food port and asked Bidart to read. Bidart turned his body so that enough light might fall on the page, and then began:

> *Suffering has made me what I am—*
> *I must not regret; or judge; or*
> *struggle to escape it*

Bidart continued reading. There was a break in the ballgame, and for a few moments, silence swelled, surrounding Bidart's pauses. Another onrush of cheering filled the block before Bidart went on:

> *There is a MORAL HERE*
> *about how LONG you must live with*
> *the consequences of a SHORT action . . .*

ten

"Love Begins Right Here in This Place"

My friend Barbara had been warning me for nearly a year about September 1988. Barbara monitored our astrological charts, and although I thought the workings of the universe were infinitely more mysterious than any system could describe, Barbara was sure I was due for major upheaval. And, I have to admit, whether the cause was Pluto square Pluto or some other conjunction, September proved to be quite a month.

Jim became assistant manager of the Arts-in-Corrections program for the entire state and moved to Sacramento to work with Bill Cleveland; Lorraine Garcia was hired to replace Jim at the prison. Jim—a man who had little need to be right or to receive credit, a man most interested in win/win situations—was a rare creature in the world of San Quentin; I admired him and had learned so much from him. Jim had seen my personal constellation of qualities and then helped me create a program in which my strengths would be maximized, thus allowing me to do the best work I'd ever done in my life. I knew I would be loyal to Jim forever.

Rumors we'd heard for a long time about San Quentin no longer remaining a maximum security institution seemed to be taking actual shape: Each week the bus brought more and more young guys facing fairly short sentences, and took away San Quentin's lifers. Spoon came to warn me he had heard he'd be one of the first lifers to be transferred. Like good old Godot, who "wasn't coming this evening, but surely tomorrow," such threats were repeated so often that Spoon—like everyone else—had learned to adopt a live-in-the-moment, just-wait-and-see state of mind. One morning, however, I walked in and saw no Spoon in the staircase. I walked to the office with a feeling of dread, and sure enough, there was a note from Spoon on my desk: "This time it's real."

Lynnelle had been ill since early summer, and late one Sunday night at the end of September, I sat in the dark by the phone listening to the news that she had died. The following week, the Point Reyes Dance Palace was filled with people who were there for Lynnelle's memorial. Young people, old people, friends from each stage of her life. One by one we spoke of our love for this woman. Some spoke of her artwork, some of aikido, some of her work in prison.

The following Wednesday, I stood in the office packing up Lynnelle's belongings to give to her husband. Above her desk was a poster a man on the Row had made for her, and I asked to keep this myself. On the heavy strip of paper were Gandhi's words: "An eye for an eye is a terrible way to blind the world."

As I put away the objects Lynnelle had gathered during her years at the prison, I was entering my last nine months at San Quentin. I felt my own sense of change and loss. Glenn and Richard had been transferred years before; Gabriel was also long gone. Jim was getting settled in Sacramento, and though Lynnelle's spirit permeated this office, she would never again sit at this desk. Spoon must, at that very moment, have been learning his way around New Folsom. The only stability—the one routine I wished *would* change—was that Elmo remained in the hole. To top it all off, my Sara had just boarded the plane that would take her away for eighteen months of travel and work in Europe.

One Monday I heard that James had been released. Hearing this broke my mood of despondency and helped me remember that change could be for the good. Those who had seen him told me that James had walked out of San Quentin dressed in a meticulously neat three-piece suit; James left the prison dignified, dapper, and free.

Many of the new young men aboard those buses pulling into San Quentin were parole violators just waiting to get back to the streets. These young toughs shocked the San Quentin old-timers. There had always been violence in the neighborhoods where most of my students had grown up, but now crack and easy access to guns had ripped these communities close to ruin. And the young men who had contributed to such destruction seemed not to care.

Over the years, some of my students had received letters about crack destroying the lives of friends, family, or women they loved. In the spring, Coties had used for his broadside a poem he called "It Use to Be Food." Lynnelle had helped Coties draw a large strawberry around this poem, which began: "What the hell is a Strawberry/I've been in jail/I don't know nuttin/bout no damn 80s slang . . . /They say it's a woman/they say she'll sell her body/ for a "Crack" to the dopeman, dopeman . . . "

"Listen, Judith," Coties said one afternoon after we had worked on this poem. "I heard Joseph Marshall from the Omega Boys Club speak on TV, and I wrote his words down: "Crack is the only thing in our history, chemical or whatever, that has been able to come between black women and the mothering process. The KKK couldn't do that. Jim Crow couldn't do that. The Old South couldn't even do that."

Coties, of course, worried about children—his children, all children—and about his people. In his poem "The Real Oakland"

Coties wrote: " . . . where Black on Black/meant Black for Blacks/not crime."

Chris explained how this decimation had been inevitable—from Chris's point of view, actually intended and ordained. Stricter sentencing laws sent adults to prison for very long stretches, so drug dealers hired kids, who had no other employment opportunities, to do much of the sales work. A kid who was picked up might face time in a juvenile facility, but not in state prison. Crack was enormously addictive and also cheap. Chris was sure the government had planted the drug in poor communities of color. Whatever the truth behind Chris's conspiracy theory, it was clear that the drug's use had spread wildly among those who had no hope for a future.

Out to dinner one night, I broke open the fortune cookie placed before me, unfolded its message, and read: "Society prepares the crime and the criminal commits it." At home, later, I looked through a group of student poems stacked on my desk for one Chris had just shown me; the fortune I'd received brought Chris's "Digested Nightmares" to mind:

> *Society carved certain paths*
> *for us to follow*
> *with nightmares disguised as truths*
>
> *we express*
> *upon a natural exhale*
> *of digested nightmares*
>
> *society scratches its ass*
> *in wonderment.*

By early fall, Coties could no longer bear what he was seeing on TV, reading in letters from home, and hearing on San Quentin's yard. He came to the office and showed me a poem that ended: "Homeboy/Homegirl/We gotta wake up/and take it all in/piece by piece/All the droppings count/cause it's your life."

"We've got to *do* something, Judith," Coties said as he looked up from reading his poem. So, at Coties's suggestion, we began work on our last class anthology: a book of poems for kids in trouble. The Gary Glassman project had been my idea, and participation had been kind-, but half-hearted. This project, however, came straight and full from Coties's considerable heart.

Each weekly shift in San Quentin's population brought some new men to our Monday night class. We no longer met in that buried basement, but in the Art Center across from Max Shack. Between the visits of guest artists and plenty of poem talk, ten men sat most Monday nights trying to find a way to speak that might catch kids' attention.

Most of these men—two whites and eight African Americans— had gone into state prison as teenagers. They wanted kids to have a different future, but they knew that youngsters would not listen to lectures from old folks. Monday after Monday these men, many of whom were likely to spend the bulk of their own lives in prison, sat around the table—an officer patrolling the gun walk outside, loud talk from the Upper Yard coming in through the transom— trying to be true to who they were and to who they had become.

What could they say? A few years after I left San Quentin, I shared poetry at a continuation high school. Many of the teenagers I worked with were already in trouble with the law, and they asked me many questions about San Quentin. No one wanted to end up in prison, but many thought it likely that they would. I asked if there was anything anyone could say that would make them change their prison-bound behavior. "No," they told me. "We have to live out our own fates."

By then, 1993, Will was the only one of my students still at San Quentin, and I'd visit him when I could. Will was a man who had taken advantage of every opportunity San Quentin offered for education and training. When he finally got out after fourteen years served, Will had indeed turned his life clear around.

After my continuation high school conversation, I visited Will and shared what the youngsters had told me. "They're right," he said. "I wouldn't have listened to anyone's advice when I was their age. But," he continued, "you still can plant seeds."

I took this image back to my students, and they nodded their heads. They talked about the positive messages adults gave them and the value these had, even when their behavior was unchanged. The kids made lists of the seeds they felt planted within them and imagined who they might be years down the road when it was time for these seeds to crack open and bloom.

Back in the fall and winter of '88–'89, my San Quentin students intuited this need for planting seeds. They knew part of the problem facing youngsters was the absence of elders. Just like the group of prisoners I'd met at that SQUIRES banquet Big Ern had invited me to more than two years before, my students cared deeply about the next generation coming up. These prisoners asked, who could better offer wise counsel than those suffering the consequences of poor choices?

I'd watched my students themselves receive such wise counsel from a guest artist, Piri Thomas. Piri, who had served seven long years in maximum security in the 1950s, had polished that jewel in the left side of his chest and earned the right to speak of luster and light. Piri, in his late fifties when he spoke to my students, served as the elder who had been through what they were now going through, and who had survived to write his classic, *Down These Mean Streets*.

As my San Quentin students set out to be elders, they began by talking about their own youth growing up. As poet Lucille Clifton put it:

> *in the inner city*
> *or*
> *like we call it*
> *home.*

As they talked, I listened. I listened to stories about little boys who had money or a jacket or the ball they'd been bouncing taken from them by another child. When such a little one told of the loss, his mother (sometimes his father, but many of my students were raised by women doing that work on their own) demanded he go back and retrieve what had been taken. These mothers knew their children lived in a war zone they would not survive if they were even once seen as a victim.

I listened to stories about other little boys who shared books with their mothers or songs or some other soft beauty. These boys learned to shelter such mothers from the truths of their son's lives on the streets. I listened to stories of little boys who learned from older ones what would be required of them to survive as men.

Protection? There was little or none. The presence of police meant harassment or worse; the police were almost always seen as agents of oppression. The boys were each other's only protectors.

Hope? Although my students now wished they had stuck more seriously with school—advice they wanted to pass on to youngsters—their own teachers and principals most often conveyed the message that these young boys were problems, not beings filled with potential. Many of my students learned from school that there was no place for them in the world beyond streets or prison.

Joy? They had each other and the neon possibilities a fast life offered.

As I sat week after week listening to my students, imagining each man as a child, I often saw the faces of actual little boys I'd been teaching in Berkeley and Oakland. One Monday night I walked out of the prison thinking of an incident that occurred just after Sara and I moved from Point Arena back to the Bay Area.

I had an after-school Poets in the Schools job with first and second graders. One little boy ran around the room each week causing havoc. DeJuan was so agitated one day that he began hitting whomever he passed as he ran through the room. The only way I could stop him from hurting another child was to put my arms around him, as gently as I could. He pushed against my arms for a moment, then settled in. And I got it: DeJuan wanted a hug.

The other six- and seven-year-olds in the room had no problem leaning up against me or climbing onto my lap. But at least at this moment, the only way DeJuan could allow himself to be hugged was to put everyone else in danger so that my arms would have to reach round him.

DeJuan finally grew calm and wanted to dictate a poem for me to write down. "Mixed with rainbow and blood" were the poem's final words.

So much talk blared on the outside about "responsibility" and "social contracts." The blather and bleating I heard over the airwaves made it hard for me—or anyone else in this society—to listen to the quiet, obvious fact I was learning: Most of my adult students had never felt part of any "social contract" more extensive than their families, immediate neighborhoods, and sometimes their race. Regardless of whatever grief they felt for those they had hurt, they felt little debt to society at large, for society at large had never invited them in. The benefits of education, job opportunity, and a sense of inclusion that even outsider-I had enjoyed never were offered to most of my students. And the time to be served spread out before them was time owed the anonymous state, not an opportunity for real restitution to those whose lives they had harmed.

So as the men worked on *The Real Rap: A Message to the Youth*, they spoke of responsibility to oneself, one's family, and one's people, but they never lost sight of the fact, as Chris would write in the book's introduction, that "responsibility is a two-way street. Each of us is individually responsible for our own life *and* society has a responsibility to all of us. For the most part, this society has not acted responsibly."

Or, as Coties put it in a poem, the system was

> . . . *y'alls precise system*
> *of laws and by-laws*
> *and in-laws and fore-fathers*

. . . I was warned
Bout y'alls
"We the People"
Cross

Still, my students tended to agree with me (though often with a pained sigh) that even if a person came into the world with racism, poverty, and every other strike there might be against him, if he didn't somehow take responsibility for his life, those forces of evil would win, and he would lose. But we all knew a child had to feel that his life counted before he could assume such responsibility, so Haki and Chuy kept reminding us that the point was not to enforce some Nancy Reagan "Just Say No" campaign, but to focus instead on what youngsters might have to say yes to: their hopes and their dreams for a place at the table with all humankind.

One afternoon during our work on *The Real Rap*, Coties walked into the office, very excited. "Did you watch *Nightline* last night?" he asked, and then answered himself, "Naw, I forgot. You don't watch TV. Well, there was what they called a national town meeting; lots of folks talking about what's dividing our cities. Mostly drag, but at the end there was this woman who said it just like it is. Get the transcript, Judith."

When the transcript arrived, Coties read Mrs. Godley's words to our class:

> I'm a mother. . . . My son passed two weeks ago when he got killed, but that's okay. That's not even the issue, that he's dead. The issue is that I have another one. And other people have sons. . . .
>
> You can open up all the jails in the world that you choose to, but if you don't get to the core of the human being that you are incarcerating, nothing is going to ever change. Nothing. Make me know that I'm worth fighting for, instead of closing the door in my damn face. . . .
>
> See, I'm one of them ones that's the foot you stepped on. I'm

187

one of them ones. You can talk that good shit. But have you felt the effects of it? Some of you all need to come down off them high horses you're up on and deal with it. . . .

You got a lot of clout, Mr. Koppel, you got a lot of clout. You understand?

You had an education, and everything. I ain't mad 'cause you had it. I have no animosity in my heart, because you had the potential to excel. I don't have that. I want the chance to excel. Make me feel like I can do it. That's what our children are asking for. I'm talking about trying to give a child, while they're young. You can take them off the porch out there and teach them that they have the potential to excel because somebody cares. Not just mouth service. The mouth will say anything, but actions don't lie.

Mrs. Godley's reminder strengthened my students' dedication to let kids know that "somebody cares." Chuy, in the poem that ended our book, claimed his, and by extension, each young reader's inherent worth:

> *. . . I am not a bad man, or a failure in the American Dream*
> *I am not a hound dog*
> *I am a man*
> *filled with emotion that has come back to me*
> *I am a good man*
> *filled with a light that gets brighter*
> *I reach further inside of myself*
> *I remember innocence, and innocence lost*
> *I remember some words from the book of life:*
> *"No man shall reach heaven unless he becomes like a child"*
> *My sense of self tells me, the answer may be simple*
> *go back to where you started*
> *go back to the dreams*
> *to the truth*

I walked into the prison one Monday in early spring and saw that main line was locked down again. This was the third Monday in a row with no class, and I was more frustrated than usual: How were we going to get the introduction to *The Real Rap* written if we couldn't meet as a group?

San Quentin had taught me nothing if it hadn't taught me the first lesson Jim passed on: "To survive and do a good job working in prison, you have to hold onto what it is you want to do and, at the very same time, let go of all assumptions that you're going to get it done in the way you first planned." So I decided to visit my students in the blocks with paper and pen; I'd ask each man what he felt we had to put in the introduction and then write his answer down as fast as I could.

In midafternoon I stood outside West Block's arched entrance, as I had so many times over the previous years, waiting for an officer to unlock the gate. After flashing my ID card and exchanging the usual banter, I again climbed that switchbacking staircase up to the third tier.

Coties was watching Oprah, and he kept the television on as he walked toward where I stood. I told him about my frustration and my decision, and I stood, pen poised, for his words. I needed to lean against something in order to write, so I moved closer to the cells than any officer would have wanted. I tried to catch the gun rail guard's eye to let him know I was conscious that I was bending the rules.

Coties talked about his youth in the projects. "We didn't have these beepers and 'Fresh Benz' kids nowadays desire," Coties began. "But we all wanted to low ride—You know what that is, Judith?—and to dress real sharp. We all wanted to have a bankroll to flash to let everybody know we were somebody. Yeah, we all wanted to be like the older brothers.

"We didn't want a robbing and stealing life for long, though. We wanted a job with General Motors or Lockheed. We wanted to settle down. I used to imagine taking my kids to the neighborhood park on Sundays, waxing my low rider, and kicking it with my high school homeboys. That's all I wanted."

I reminded Coties about a conversation we'd had soon after I'd begun teaching at San Quentin. Coties had brought a poem to that class session three years before. In it he described being put in prison for a crime he didn't commit. As we talked about the poem, Coties told us that he'd done plenty of petty crimes and was known by the police in his neighborhood. They could never pin anything on him, though, so when this big crime occurred, they gleefully accused him.

At first, Coties told us, he wasn't worried because he knew he was nowhere around the scene of the crime. But then someone who had been there identified him. Coties said he went into shock; how could this be happening to him?

That evening in class, someone had called out, "Coties, stop your sniveling."

I didn't think Coties was sniveling, but the poem he showed us talked of the bum rap without telling the whole story. When I mentioned this, many of the men explained to me that when they were youngsters, "guilt" meant getting caught. If you weren't caught, you weren't guilty. At first I, with my born-and-bred middle-class ethical values, thought, "Well, *that's* sure convenient." But as I listened more deeply, I realized that what I was hearing was not mere expedient self-interest, but an actual way of seeing the world.

In West Block, I reminded Coties of that poem, "My Justice Spill," and said I thought we should include the final draft he'd written. Coties went to the box under his cot, pulled out a copy, and began reading:

> . . . *I thought I was cool*
> *Going to school & work*
> *And robbing on the side*
> *not caring about the victims*
> *I was getting ahead*
> *on the man's "Student Loans and Grants"*
> *and "Sticking em up on the Streets"*
> *getting caught*

being freed
on the victim's lack of eyesight alone

But I was on a mystic voyage
of miscues
Mishaps
of judgments . . .

Now I'm here
not caught for what I did do
pinned for what I didn't
and suffering for them both.

I left Coties's cell and walked down the tier to speak with the rest of my students. Smokey spoke of his own son and urged that the introduction focus on our concern for the kids; Lateef and Eddie stressed education; Curtis talked of the lure of drugs, and Stretch of the power of imagination. Chris wanted to make sure we emphasized the growing inequality of society and how such inequality breeds violence and crime. Will handed me a poem he thought could serve as an epigraph to the introduction, with its reminder to the kids that, "We've been where you're going."

At home I typed up the notes I'd scribbled. As I typed, I thought I'd conveyed the men's thoughts, but not their language. I knew this was a fatal flaw, since the men had worked so hard to find words kids might listen to. I took copies of what I had typed to each student and asked for heavy edits.

Elmo had been in the hole while we were working on this project; he had no poems in the book. But by spring, Elmo was out, and he took on the primary task of rewriting the introduction so that the words had the greatest chance of being effective. When I read the final version to the men in class, we all felt proud:

> We are ten men who are serving time at San Quentin State Prison. Some of us could be here for the rest of our lives. We have put together this book in an effort to ask you youngsters coming

up to please look at yourselves and the world around you and make very careful choices about how you want to live your lives.

. . . We know, from our lives' hard experiences, that we must speak what's real, speak from our hearts to yours. We think we've learned from our experiences what the real world is about. So instead of staring at the walls, we write poems and stories about our youth and our lives in prison, about what we've learned and what we love, about the dreams we forgot and those that keep us alive. . . .

The first thing you need to know is that the cards are stacked against you. That's real. If you get caught up in drugs and crime, you're playing a game you just can't win. Most everyone in prison agrees that, "Everyone I know who was getting in trouble when I was coming up, is either dead or in the pen."

If you're poor, or live in a bad neighborhood, or your parents are irresponsible, or everywhere you look you see people using drugs or involved in gangs, the cards are stacked against you. . . . You gotta play the hand you were dealt or you lose before you ever get the chance to see what life is all about.

. . . It is the nature of youth to enjoy life and to live for the moment, but we have learned at great cost the consequences of this behavior. *We* are the reality—men locked up in prison—and we're here to tell you that everything you do has consequences, consequences for the lives of those you take from and hurt; consequences for those you love who have to witness the harm you are doing to yourself and others. You might feel you are "man enough" to accept whatever consequences come your way, but the real question is whether you are man enough to choose a better way of life that will lead to positive consequences for yourself and the society as a whole.

In the neighborhood, it's all about being hip, being cool and having the right image. Everything is surface. It's all about how you are perceived by others. But we never learn to look beyond that, never learn to be about what we feel on the inside. Be it because of peer pressure, or the desire to project a certain image, young people are seldom encouraged to express their real feelings, their dreams and fears about their futures, about what they want from life. Many of us have kids of our own and we want them to develop their own naturally given gifts and abilities. We want our children (and *all* children) to feel free to dream about being doctors and scientists without having to feel pressure to be hip or loyal to the criminal influences around them. We want them to know themselves, their true selves, before they get caught up in what others want to teach them. Because we *know* how it is: we all listened to a lot of bad advice from corrupt sources. We looked up to the pimps and players and gamblers and thieves and dope dealers. Whoever was "getting over" and not getting caught.

But now we try to see our heroes differently. We see poor people fighting to regain their neighborhoods from the killing effects of drug abuse and we applaud them. It takes real courage to stand up against the dope pushers and the gang bangers that pervade so many poor communities and steal from them any hope for a better standard of living. It is the people engaged in that struggle who are the real heroes.

. . . Together the ten of us have served almost one hundred years behind these walls, so we don't have to prove how tough we are to anyone. We've survived our years in prison with pride and have each come to possess an ever growing sense of what it really takes to make it in this world. What we have to say to you now is that it's easy to take the easy way out—hustling all day every day for that easy money, the cheap sex and another notch on your belt. But, in the end, where does that get you? What really counts is the struggle because you only get out of life what you're willing to put into it. It's all about the sacrifice: what has come to you as a result of putting forth your best effort.

And so we say to you, think of the world as your future, for it is. The universe is yours and it's as limitless as your potential. You can be anything you dare to be; all you have to do is try. Don't blow it, man.

You might see poverty and racism and violence all around you, but that doesn't mean you have to be a part of it. If things are so bad, work to change them. Hold on to your dreams and be true to them; be true to yourself.

Too many young people are forced to live in poverty, subject to discrimination, racism, etc. . . . Be responsible for yourself *and* demand social responsibility from those who run the government.

And remember that your dreams are not only for yourself. Some day you will be fathers, mothers, grandparents. Someday you'll look back on where you came from and we hope you can tell your children and grandchildren that you were part of the solution and not part of the problem. Maybe your parents weren't able to do that for you, but that doesn't mean you can't make things better in your own life and, in some way, for your children's children's children. We hope some day you can tell your children and grandchildren with pride, "I was part of that." Not part of an Oakland or Bayview–Hunters Point that turned out drug addicts and men serving life in prison and derelict bums on street corners, but turned out instead scientists, athletes, good mechanics, musicians, bus drivers, teachers, construction workers, crossing guards, community workers, preachers—men and women we can look up to; men and women nourishing, not wasting, their talent; men and women who change the world.

When the book came back from the printer, I sent copies to over four hundred schools, juvenile facilities, and community programs. So many requests came in for additional copies that the warden asked San Quentin's print shop to prepare a second printing.

Of course I was pleased; my students had worked hard on this project. Their months-long effort to be true both to their memories of the youngsters they had been *and* to their desire that other young folk avoid their own harsh fates seemed noble to me.

That long ago night when I'd brought in Hikmet's poem and asked my bumbling question—"What can you do, even in prison, so that the jewel in the left side of your chest doesn't lose its luster?"—I had actually thought my students could compose a reply. They knew, however, the only worthy response was the one that they lived. For nearly four years, I'd been privileged to observe some of their day-by-day answers.

Soon after I'd come to the prison, Elmo recommended I read Daniel Berrigan's *Lights On in the House of the Dead*. Berrigan, a Jesuit priest who served time in prison because of his antiwar activities in the '60s, wrote: "It remains important that prison be regarded as a boot camp for spiritual change."

In the face of a system that saw them as monsters, prisoners had to find ways to remain human and remember that they were—as Coties had put it in those lines I'd loved all these years—"that intricate part/missing from the whole." Righteous proclamations of their humanity were easy; the proof was revealed in how a man responded moment by moment to a life designed to rob even a saint of all dignity and self-respect.

More than one man told me that every night, before falling asleep, he reviewed the day, scanning for people he might have offended or anger he might have expressed without thinking. This activity informed a man where danger might lie, but went beyond such self-protection. As I listened to descriptions of this ritual, I heard of a nightly effort to clear a man's relations with others, to learn to let go, and to discover how to transmute negative feelings into forgiveness.

One afternoon Peter arrived at the Arts-in-Corrections office shaking his head. He'd just been up on the Row with art supplies. In one cell a student sat in the dark, drawing. When Peter asked, the man told him the cell's light bulb had burned out a few days before, but no guard had replaced the bulb. With no way to get light, the man drew in the dark.

For ten months of Wednesdays I'd visited Elmo in East Block. Each time I walked in, my senses were assaulted by loud noise, foul smells, stacked trash, and general bleakness. Though all of me cringed before I made my way up to the tier, I knew what I experienced was the tiniest fraction of what Elmo once described as "that hatred like hands in the way it touched me at times." There was no way in the world I could channel enough light to illuminate East Block.

Each week I watched Elmo do what was necessary to keep his mind, body, and spirit in shape. I wasn't Elmo's therapist or priest; I just tried to be a warm and bright presence in the cold darkness of East Block. I assumed that if I landed in some four-and-one-half-by-eleven-foot cell for twenty-three hours a day, every day for ten months, I'd let myself sink into a pit of despair I'd never be able to return from, so I was all the more in awe of Elmo's determination to keep his soul alive.

For the years I'd known Will, he always had a release date—fall 1993. Will set his sight on that date and paced himself accordingly, taking advantage of every class, training program, and job that San Quentin offered. His goal was to be prepared so that when he hit the streets, he'd easily find a good job and a satisfying life.

In 1992, Will received a letter: "Sorry, we figured your time wrong. You'll get out in '94." Will had barely absorbed this sick twist when another letter arrived: "Oops, we mean '95."

Even my well-developed imagination could not summon what it would be to face this fate. But Will took quite a few deep breaths, readjusted his pacing, and stayed focused on his goal: getting out and having a life.

When Piri Thomas came in as a "wise elder" guest artist, he told my students—those walk smooth young toughs—that during his own seven years down in New York, he'd awakened one night hearing someone cry out, "Mami, Mami!" He jerked around to see where those cries had come from and realized it had been he, Piri, calling out in the dark for his mother. Piri said that night after night, during those seven long years, he would stroke his heart before falling asleep. He demonstrated in front of the room filled with San Quentin long-termers how he had turned his face to kiss first his right shoulder, then his left, giving himself the warmth, kindness, and love he knew he needed to survive.

Sometimes, someone else broke through to touch my students as human beings rather than convicts. The kids in Point Arena did that for Spoon. The kids' poems shone so brightly, Spoon was able to take *off* his shades. These poems took him, as he later wrote, "beyond the walls of San Quentin" and made him truly feel "like a poet." Although the prison system demanded Spoon remember that from the institution's perspective, he was an inmate before he was a man, Spoon responded by writing a poem.

In Borofsky and Glassman's video *Prisoner*, James talked of a wild kid who'd once been his cell mate. The kid talked to James and "he would tell me certain things and he wouldn't hear it from anyone else. In other words," James said on the tape, "what he told me stayed with me. He started to tell me more things, and I got to understand him.

"At first he couldn't read; I taught him to read, got him interested in books and learning about himself, and about how to deal with people. He's grown from a wild, silly, violent, unfeeling, immature child into a man.

"He just got transferred Thursday, and the change between when I met him and what he is now is like the difference between day and night. And he told me something that made me feel so good, that if we hadn't been standing in the yard, I probably would have cried. He said, 'Being in the cell with you is the best thing that ever happened to me.' I mean, I can't tell you how that made me feel, that I'd done something. Here in this place, where there is absolutely nothing good to do, I'd done some good."

In May 1987, Mother Teresa visited San Quentin. She spoke at the Catholic chapel and said, "Love begins right here in this place." This love was the ground for my students' ability to maintain that jewel's luster; love was the ground for the vision of wholeness I hungered after; love was the ground that, for four years, together we "disguised as a poem," as Elmo had put it. There was the actual human love I felt for Elmo, Spoon, Chris, Coties, Will,

James, and all the men whose lives had touched mine, even Gabriel. And also Love, the love Mother Teresa referred to when she asked us to, "Please recognize the God in each other."

When I'd been at the prison only a few months, I had a vision—more sight than sensation—of wanting to take all the men into my body. At first this shocked me, but I soon saw the impulse wasn't sexual. When I was two and one-half and my father told me about the death of my infant brother (that moment I first sensed myself inside my skin), I had invited my brother's spirit in with me. That little girl wanted to be a home for her bodiless brother.

A similar desire fueled this adult vision: I saw my skin as the place where these men's battles ended. And though I loved each individual man, it was not my love making a haven, but Love coming through me.

Each morning as I walked that long walk into the prison, Jewish me repeated the Saint Francis prayer:

> Lord, make me a channel of your peace.
> Where there is hatred, let me sow love;
> where there is injury, pardon;
> where there is despair, hope;
> where there is darkness, light;
> and where there is sadness, joy . . .

Elmo once compared me to Mr. Magoo, "oblivious to so much, yet ever unscathed by it. 'And David chose five smooth stones from the river,'" Elmo quoted, saying my innocence was my five smooth stones and "the most potent and effective weapon in the face of the giant that was all the hatred and violence and deceit that was at work all around you."

I was incredibly moved by this description. But I also knew that I'd consciously chosen innocence. Not the ignorant "false innocence" I did my best to avoid, but rather an innocence that *desired* to look at San Quentin through the eyes of Love.

Of course, during most of the moments I lived through at the prison, I was my small little self, hurt or made happy by Elmo, wary of Gabriel, laughing with Spoon, annoyed by or in awe of this man or that. But there were moments when Spoon handed me a poem, or Elmo a lesson, and the world around us cracked open and I could see—as I'd prayed to—the whole of which we were each only part.

In *The Real Rap*, my students planted seeds out of the love they felt for the next generation coming up. They had not the slightest assurance their words would make one drop of difference. Still, they spent month after month struggling to speak from their hearts. Chris once told me, "The System uses up good people like you." My students' words might have no effect; my attempts to "channel peace" might be in vain, but my students and I knew love was the human gift we had to give, and we did our best to give it.

June 26 would be our last Monday night class. I'd asked for, and received, permission to have a small party. For days I'd casually asked the six students remaining in class (after a flurry of transfers) what desserts they liked best. "Pecan pie," Smokey said. "Anything chocolate," Chris told me. "Really subtle, Judith," Elmo smiled.

But Elmo happily joined the others eating the pies, cookies, and cakes I had baked. The men told me, now that this grant was over, I should go work with kids *before* they come to prison—employment advice I would follow.

In the following weeks, every man in the room except Will would be transferred to another state prison. The group we'd created together for close to four years would disappear. But the poems—and the love that they sprang from—would be part of our lives forever.

notes

Disguised as a Poem

In Birkenstocks and hand-crafted earrings
still living a life from the sixties
you enter this place
this dungeon
this dust bowl on the edge of the bay
where 3,000 men wait
for the sweet rain called freedom.

You walk a path from the front gate
across the garden plaza
Your pale feet step softly
upon the spots where angry men have died
Don't let the pink and yellow roses fool you
This is not a pretty place.

Two flights down
you wait for us to come
bearing the fruits and scars of our embattled lives
disguised as poems
scrawled on bits of paper

last week
in a cell
when sleep was hard to find.

For three hours in that basement room
we are cut off
A million miles away
from your daughter and your cat
A hundred yards from death row.

For three hours
we joust
we orbit around each other wrestling with words
we make love with words
we grow close
We meet in a place called poetry
one woman
and a few captured men
We speak of poems
and grasp at them like straws
until it is time to go.

Two flights up
the cool night air greets us
There are always those few tight minutes
waiting for count to clear
and the inevitable parting of ways
We could go have coffee and speak of poems all night
but your daughter will miss you
and I must be back in my cell before ten.

It is always the same
For three hours
you or Phavia or Sharon or Scoop
manage to get close to me
only to be peeled away
like the bark from a young tree
leaving behind a little spot
bare and vulnerable
that does not want to see you go
but will die of exposure
long before you return.
    —Elmo Chattman, Jr.

Preface

IX Black Bart was a late-nineteenth-century highwayman who robbed stage-coaches, often leaving a poem at the scene of the crime. One such missive read:

I've labored long for bread
For honor and for riches,
But on my corns too long you've tread
You fine haired Sons of Bitches
   —Black Bart the PO8

For more information, see George Hoeper, *Black Bart: Boulevardier Bandit* (Fresno, Calif.: Word Dancer Press, 1995).

IX George Jackson, whose letters are collected in *Soledad Brother: The Prison Letters of George Jackson* (New York: Coward-McCann, 1970), was killed at San Quentin.

IX "As befitting a myth . . . ": Kenneth Lamott, *Chronicles of San Quentin: The Biography of a Prison* (New York: David McKay Co., 1961). See also Clinton T. Duffy, *The San Quentin Story*, as told to Dean Jennings (Garden City, N.Y.: Doubleday, 1950), for the experiences of the man who was warden at San Quentin during the 1940s.

X In 1975, Eloise Smith was the director of the newly formed California Arts Council (CAC). As part of her research into arts activity throughout California, she visited the prisons at Soledad and Vacaville.

The CAC established its Artists in Social Institutions program in 1976. At that time Smith, no longer director of the CAC, and her husband, the writer and historian Page Smith, designed a three-year pilot Prison Arts Project for the Vacaville facility. Through their nonprofit organization, the William James Association, the Smiths applied for grants for this program, which began in 1977 and met with great success.

During the California legislature's 1980–81 budget hearings, Senator Henry Mello introduced a $400,000 augmentation to the California Department of Corrections' annual budget, to be used specifically for arts programming. By November 1981, there were artist/facilitators at six California prisons and eighteen artists teaching under the auspices of Arts-in-Corrections. In 1999, there were artist/facilitators and active art programs at all of California's thirty-three prisons.

In the 1960s, before Arts-in-Corrections, San Quentin held annual arts and crafts shows, which brought as many as ten thousand citizens to San Quentin's outer grounds. (In 1960, visitors paid $8,000 for paintings, sculpture, and handicrafts.) Warden Fred R. Dickson said of the annual event, "They help break down the walls and let the people out-side know what kind of people we have in here. This is a community like any other community, except that the men are locked up." Lamott, *Chronicles of San Quentin*, p. 263.

XI An excellent collection of writing by men and women in prison is *Prison Writing in 20th-Century America*, edited by H. Bruce Franklin (New York: Penguin Books, 1998).

XII Bill Cleveland, *Art in Other Places: Artists at Work in America's Community and Social Institutions* (Westport, Conn.: Praeger, 1992).

XII In "New Deal Art Projects: Boondoggle or Bargain?" (*Art News*, April 1982), Milton I. Brown writes about the two independent art projects operating from 1935 to 1943. One of these was under the Treasury Department, which was responsible for building and maintaining all federal buildings. The second program was under the Works Progress Administration (WPA) and consisted of four units: Art, Writers, Theater, and Music. Since government patronage of the arts during the Depression was tied to FDR's New Deal (designed to put the unemployed back to work), when times got better economically, funding for the arts decreased.

The Comprehensive Employment and Training Act (CETA) was operative from 1974 to 1983. During those years, CETA funded six hundred art projects in two hundred localities, employing five thousand artists and another five thousand arts-associated staff. Large numbers of artists were introduced to schools, senior centers, and other social service environments through work under CETA. CETA's funding was also tied to the employment rate: As unemployment went down, funds were cut off. (Interview with John Kreidler, former Arts and Humanities program executive at the San Francisco Foundation.)

Another historical root of the community arts field is the Highlander Research and Education Center in Tennessee. Begun in 1932 by Myles Horton, this folk school was central to the training of civil rights workers in the 1950s and 1960s and the place where the version of "We Shall Overcome" that we sing today was born. (For more information about Highlander, see Myles Horton, *Long Haul: An Autobiography*, with Judith Kohl and Herbert Kohl (New York: Doubleday, 1990); Bud Schultz and Ruth Schultz, *It Did Happen Here* (Berkeley: University of California Press, 1989); and *We Shall Overcome: Songs of the Southern Freedom Movement* (New York: Oak Publications, 1963).

For further discussion and examples of artists who are engaged, rather than alienated, and of art as a process that has the power to address social concerns, see Suzi Gablik, *Has Modernism Failed?* (New York: Thames and Hudson, 1984) and *The Re-enchantment of Art* (New York: Thames and Hudson, 1991), as well as Mat Schwarzman and Mark

O'Brien, editors, *Reimaging America: The Art of Social Change* (Philadelphia: New Society Publishers, 1990).

XII "There's increasing pressure now to prove": Beth spoke these words in a presentation before the California Arts Council in 1987. In fact, Arts-in-Corrections *has* been shown to lower the recidivism rate. The Brewster Report (1987) showed that prisoners who participated in Arts-in-Corrections programs for at least six months had a rate of return reduced by 51 percent compared to the California prison population at large.

Research conducted by the California Department of Corrections and the Law Enforcement Assistance Administration indicates that prisoners involved in ongoing arts programs show a 70 to 80 percent reduction in violent and other disruptive behavior while in prison and are 40 percent less likely to return to prison once released.

In the final report of the California Task Force to Promote Self-Esteem and Personal and Social Responsibility (submitted to the California Legislature in January 1990), Recommendation 8 in the "Crime and Violence and Self-Esteem" section advises: "Support arts programs in institutional settings. . . . The learning and practice of art requires patience, commitment, self-discipline, imagination, and an attitude of cooperation.

"To master an arts discipline, one grows in self-confidence and acquires a feeling of competence. These attributes make programs in the visual, literary, and performing arts particularly effective for incarcerated individuals.

"In acquiring artistic skills, participants learn to affect their environment in a constructive manner. For some, learning a creative process also produces a fundamental change in attitude about themselves and others."

XII "Condemning violence is . . .": James Gilligan, *Violence: Our Deadly Epidemic and Its Causes* (New York: G.P. Putnam, 1996).

XIII Stories repeated over time become a mythology—part factual history, part belief system, part poetic expression. Mythologies govern how we perceive what is in front of our eyes. At San Quentin I heard stories about prisoners whose wives smuggled in drugs taped inside baby diapers, stories about prisoners who removed steel from their bed frames and buried it in their shoes until they were on the yard and able to make a hit. Such stories led guards to repeat, "They're all assholes."

I also heard stories about guards who taunted prisoners until they couldn't take any more, blew up, and were escorted to the hole. Repeated stories about guards who arbitrarily and cruelly exercised their authority resulted in prisoners spitting "K9!" after any man in green.

Teaching artists told stories, too. There was one about a prisoner at the Northern California Women's Facility who made a puppet in the image of a sweet girl in a bonnet. When the bonnet was taken off, though, the back of this puppet's head was gray, distorted, and hideous. "That's the childhood she must hide," the prisoner explained.

Then there was the story of a guitarist at Soledad, in class the first night, playing elaborate chords and progressions.

"This is a *beginning* class," the teaching artist said.

"This is the first time I've picked up a guitar," the prisoner answered.

"Impossible," said the teacher.

"It's true," the man said. "I was in the hole in Folsom for over ten years. I made a neck out of cardboard and got myself some chord books. That's how I learned to play. This is the first time I'm hearing how it sounds."

one

4 "Prison can make you or break you": George Jackson, *Soledad Brother.* For one account of George Jackson's death at San Quentin, see Paul Liberatore, *The Road to Hell: The True Story of George Jackson, Stephen Bingham, and the San Quentin Massacre* (New York: Atlantic Monthly Press, 1996).

6 For more information on the Omega Boys Club, see Joseph Marshall, *Street Soldier: One Man's Struggle to Save a Generation, One Life at a Time* (New York: Delacorte Press, 1996).

7 "Some men claimed 'diminished capacity' . . . ": San Francisco's infamous Dan White, who killed Mayor George Moscone and Supervisor Harvey Milk in front of witnesses, received a reduced sentence using what came to be called the "Twinkie defense."

8 Life sentences in California prior to November 1978 were "seven years-to-life" (compared with the current "twenty-five-to-life"). Many men convicted in the 1970s continue to be denied parole by the Board of Prison Terms, before which they must appear. In fact, according to the *San Jose Mercury News* (December 17, 1995) and the Board of Prison Terms' 1988 Life Prisoner Report, the average number of lifers granted parole declined from 6.2 percent in the years 1983–1988 to .82 percent in 1994. On October 3, 1999, the *Los Angeles Times* reported that in 1999, on average, .5 percent were granted parole by the board. The governor blocked the thirteen parole grants the board sent him for review during that year.

Pratt's conviction was eventually overturned and he was released from prison in June 1997.

9 Mt. Tamalpais is a presence in this landscape. There is no final agreement on where the name came from, whether it is of Coast Miwok or Spanish origin, or whether from some combination of the two. I'd often hike on Mt. Tam and sometimes, since my route to the mountain

took me by San Quentin, I'd stop at the prison for a short while to take care of one small task or another. (On such days, I'd have to hike in pants other than shorts or jeans—both of which I was forbidden to wear inside the institution.) Often I'd see some of my students as I dashed in and out. I'd tell them to look up to the mountain in an hour or so, for I'd be there then, looking down at San Quentin, thinking of them.

13 T.M. is Transcendental Meditation. Volunteers from many organizations came into the prison to offer "self-help groups" to interested prisoners.

14 "The Protocols of the Learned Elders of Zion" is the most notorious and successful work of modern anti-Semitism. A late nineteenth-century edition was created by agents of the Okhrana (Russian secret police) in Paris, based on a satire written by Maurice Joly in 1864 and developed by Hermann Goedsche, writing under the name of Sir John Retcliffe, into an alleged account of a Jewish conspiracy. "The Protocols" made its way back to Russia and became part of a propaganda campaign, which accompanied the pogroms of 1905. By the 1920s, there was a book as well as many articles documenting the fabrication, but "The Protocols" continued to circulate widely and was even sponsored by Henry Ford in the United States until 1927. It formed an important part of the Nazi's justification of genocide of the Jews in World War II.

14 In the following weeks, I lent Coties Bernard Malamud's *The Assistant;* he found this story of a Jewish shopkeeper and his world very moving.

17 Jack Henry Abbott, *In the Belly of the Beast: Letters from Prison* (New York: Random House, Vintage Books, 1981).

17 "I read from Joe Morse's editorial": Editorial, *San Quentin News*, October 24, 1986.

19 "Some Advice to Those Who Will Serve Time in Prison," from *Nazim Hikmet: Selected Poetry*, translated by Randy Blasing and Mutlu Konuk (New York: Persea Books, 1994).

21 Larry McInnerney asked me to read at Tehachapi. I give so much thanks to Larry and his partner, Rojelio Carlos, for the poetry-performance work we did together as well as for all I learned from them over the years.

21 When some older Californians hear "Tehachapi," they still think of the women's prison. The state's few women prisoners were incarcerated at San Quentin until a separate facility was built at Tehachapi in 1933. The women moved to the California Institution for Women when it was built in 1952. There are currently four women's prisons in the state.

two

27 Michael Hogan, "A Prison Workshop in Arizona," *American Poetry Review* (January/February 1976).

28   *Playing for Time* was originally a movie made for television. It was adapted by Arthur Miller from the memoir written by Fania Fenelon, a survivor of Auschwitz.

29   "If the doors of perception were cleansed every thing would appear to man as it is, infinite," William Blake wrote in *The Marriage of Heaven and Hell* (1793), that ode to contraries whose last line declares: "For every thing that lives is Holy."

29   "Accustom the public": Robert Bresson, *Notes on Cinematography*, translated by Jonathan Griffin (New York: Urizen Books, 1977).

30   "Do I contradict myself?": Walt Whitman, "Song of Myself."

30   "The test of a first-rate intelligence": F. Scott Fitzgerald, *The Crack Up.*

30   "When man is capable": John Keats, Letter, December 22, 1817.

31   "Men I admired and cared for": In *Father Greg and the Homeboys: The Extraordinary Journey of Father Greg Boyle and His Work with the Latino Gangs of East L.A.* (New York: Hyperion, 1995), p. 68, author Celeste Fremon reports: "'Dreamer is a wonderful, wonderful kid,' Greg says, as the light of the day fades. 'And he shot a little girl. A lot of people can't hold those two thoughts together. But the task of a true human being is to do precisely that.'"

31   "Bobo's Metamorphosis" and other poems by Milosz can be found in Czeslaw Milosz, *The Collected Poems* (New York: Ecco Press, 1988).

31   Carolyn Forché, "The Colonel," from *The Country between Us* (New York: Harper & Row, 1981).

31   "The blood of the children": In "A Few Things Explained," from Pablo Neruda, *Residence on Earth* (translated by Frances Mayes in *The Discovery of Poetry* [New York: Harcourt Brace Jovanovich, 1987]). In their original Spanish, the lines are: *"y por las calles la sangre de los niños/corria simplemente, como sangre de niños."*

34   San Quentin and Folsom were both built in the nineteenth century (San Quentin in 1852 and Folsom in 1880), and they are the only two prisons in California whose cells have open bars and whose cell block tiers are stacked five high. (This design is prevalent in older prisons elsewhere in the country.) California Institution for Men, in Chino, was built in 1941 and also has open bars, but only three tiers.

   The original women's prison at Tehachapi—now California Correctional Institution—was built in 1933. Eight prisons were built between 1945 and 1965: California Training Facility, Soledad, in 1946; California Institution for Women in 1952; Deuel Vocational Institution in 1953; California Men's Colony in 1954; California Medical Facility in 1955; California Rehabilitation Center in 1962; California Correctional Center in 1963; and Sierra Conservation Center in 1965. Most cells in these prisons have solid doors, and no block is more than three tiers high. There were no prisons built in California between 1966 and 1984, but in the following thirteen years, twenty-one new prisons opened.

40 "The population of U.S prisons": Under California's 1994 "Three Strikes" sentencing law, the mandatory sentence for a "third strike" is twenty-five-to-life. According to a March 1996 report from the Center on Juvenile and Criminal Justice (which quoted California Department of Corrections statistics), in California African Americans are currently arrested for felonies at 4.7 times the rate of whites, incarcerated at 7.8 times the rate of whites, and imprisoned for a "third strike" at 13.3 times the rate of whites. Nearly four in ten of the state's young black males are under some form of sentence. (Christopher Davis, Richard Estes, and Vincent Schiraldi, *Three Strikes: The New Apartheid* [San Francisco: The Center on Juvenile and Criminal Justice].)

41 "Martial Arts" is from Phavia Kujichagulia, *Undercover or Overexposed* (Oakland, Calif.: A. Wisdom Company, 1989).

44 Here are the writers who visited our class as guest artists: Kim Addonizio, Opal Palmer Adisa, Frank Bidart, D. F. Brown, Rojelio Carlos, Wanda Coleman, Sharon Doubiago, Kate Doughterty, Norman Fischer, Jack and Adele Foley, Richard Garcia, Ruth Gendler, Paula Gocker, Herb Gold, Grady Hillman, Barbara Jamison, Kiva, Dawn Kolokithas, Phavia Kujichagulia, Dorianne Laux, Genny Lim, Devorah Major, Malcolm Margolin, Czeslaw Milosz, Sharman Murphy, Wes "Scoop" Nisker, Orville Schell, Laura Schiff, Kim Shelton, Rosalie Sorrels, Joan Swift, Beth Thielan, Piri Thomas, and Mike Tuggle.

In addition to receiving these guest artists, we watched dozens of poetry readings on videotape. These came from The American Poetry Archives at San Francisco State University's Poetry Center (1600 Holloway Avenue, San Francisco, California 94132), a fabulous resource for anyone teaching any form of creative writing.

Since my years teaching at San Quentin, the Lannan Foundation, a private contemporary arts organization, has produced a series of literary videotapes featuring major poets and writers from around the globe reading and talking about their work. These tapes are available from the American Poetry Archives. The Foundation can be contacted at 313 Read Street, Santa Fe, New Mexico 87501-2628.

t h r e e

50 "Paul Minicucci": During the years of its existence, the state legislature's Joint Committee on the Arts acted as a policy forum and oversight committee for state art agencies, including the California Arts Council and Arts-in-Corrections. Paul described his vision (in an interview with the author): "In the late seventies I was visited by cultural counselors

from Germany. These artists opened my eyes to the fact that art is the ultimate neighborhood activity. In Germany—and in many European countries—arts funding is given for a contract between the artist and the community. If an artist is needed in the schools, the artist goes there; if a mural's needed, the artist works on that. In France, an *animateur* goes into a community to do a play with residents that takes as its subject the social needs of that particular town. When an artist is part of a community, you don't have to defend arts programming. Everyone knows the artists and the work they're doing. It's part of daily life and no one wants to lose that."

50 "For three days I listened to": Joe Bruchac's Greenfield Review Press published much prison writing in the 1970s and early '80s, including *The House of the Dead: A Kite from Soledad* in 1971 and *Light from Another Country: Poetry from American Prisons* in 1984. Grady Hillman is a poet and the first-ever resident artist in the Texas prison system. Laurie Meadoff founded the CityKids Foundation in 1984. The foundation involves young people in creating and managing events and activities that promote youth-to-youth and youth-to-adult communication. Liz Lerman is a dancer and choreographer who has worked with seniors, forming a company called the Dancers of the Third Age. Rebecca Rice is an actress, writer, singer, poet, and teacher who has worked at "giving voice to the invisible people," as she said in her talk. Her own work has been deeply influenced by the lives of those she has taught. Judy Baca is the founder of the Social and Public Arts Resource Center (SPARC). Baca has initiated many mural projects in which she works with a multiracial group of teenagers, fifty to eighty strong.

56 During my four years at San Quentin, others teaching through Arts-in-Corrections at the prison included Peter Carpou (visual art), Malonga Casquelourd (drumming), Aida de Arteaga (music), Sara Felder (juggling and circus arts), Stephen Herrick (music), Drew Klausner (animation), Lynnelle (visual art), Patrick Maloney (visual art), and Floyd Salas (poetry).

58 "Why was the little shoe": Jim often told such jokes, but I have my niece and nephew, Emma and Gus Ingebretsen, to thank for this one.

58 As of November 1, 1999, there are 555 prisoners on Death Row in California, according to the California Department of Corrections.

62 When Lynnelle talked about her own emotional struggles sharing art with her condemned students, she spoke in the language of those quotes I'd tacked to my wall. She said (in an interview with the author), "In my relationship with these men, they are warm, outgoing, light, appreciative, and loving people. On the other hand, there is the knowledge of what they have done. And I have never been able to resolve that. All I do is hold these truths in both hands and just look at both sides."

Because she worked on Death Row, Lynnelle was frequently asked for interviews. Often reporters asked, "Why do these people deserve art? Look at what they have done."

Lynnelle told me she didn't have an easy answer. "It's not like my students are going to be back on the streets and so should have something positive that they can find out about themselves before they are returned to the community. No, my students are going to die. Why do they deserve art? My belief system says we are here on this earth for a purpose, and part of it is the progression of our soul or our spirit, and what we do with our life here has some positive or negative effect and art is a very positive way to look at yourself and to touch your spirit. It is very important that people in society know that these people have something to offer, that they are not all bad, that there is another side, that perhaps they may have to be always locked up, but they at least have a potential to put something into society that's good."

A book that examines similar issues regarding men on Death Row is Sister Helen Prejean's *Dead Man Walking: An Eyewitness Account of the Death Penalty in the United States* (New York: Random House, 1993).

four

65 "You Gotta Walk": The title is from Woody Guthrie's "Lonesome Valley."
68 *Poetry Flash* is a poetry review and literary calendar for the western Unites States. The paper is distributed free in bookstores and cafés throughout the area. Subscriptions can be obtained from *Poetry Flash*, 1450 Fourth Street #4, Berkeley, California 94710.
70 "I thought of the Joe Morse editorial": Editorial, *San Quentin News*, October 3, 1986.
72 "For among these winters": Rainer Maria Rilke, *Sonnets to Orpheus*, translated by Stephen Mitchell (New York: Simon and Schuster, 1985).
73 Robert Bly, editor, *News of the Universe: Poems of Twofold Consciousness* (San Francisco: Sierra Club Books, 1980).
79 Rainer Maria Rilke, *Letters to a Young Poet*, translated by Stephen Mitchell (New York: Random House, Vintage Books, 1986).

five

81 "A production of . . . *Waiting for Godot*": All quotes from the play in this and subsequent chapters are from Samuel Beckett, *Waiting for Godot* (New York: Grove Press, 1954).

82 "Godot at San Quentin": from Martin Esslin, *The Theatre of the Absurd* (London: Methuen, 1961).

82 "It was an expression": *San Quentin News*, November 1957.

82 "Rick Cluchey gained a pardon": Rick Cluchey's life was the basis for the 1987 movie *Weeds*, directed by John Hancock and starring Nick Nolte.

91 "What we choose to fight": Rainer Maria Rilke, "The Man Watching." From *News of the Universe*.

six

100 The chapter title is from Czeslaw Milosz's "*Ars Poetica?*"

103 A catalogue of Les Blank's films and videos is available from Flower Films and Video, 10341 San Pablo Avenue, El Cerrito, California 94530; phone (510) 525-0942; fax (510) 525-1204.

104– "To prove that prison was a dangerous place": In late 1996, the *San Fran-*
105 *cisco Chronicle* ran a series of articles indicating that top corrections officials had requested billions of dollars in additional funds from the state legislature, citing increased prison violence as a justification. At the same time, however, prison guards were pitting convicts against each other in hand-to-hand combat in the SHU units at Corcoran State Prison and betting on the outcomes (and shooting more than fifty prisoners, seven of whom died). These events were reported through the chain of command by a Corcoran guard and lieutenant, but their complaints were not dealt with. Eventually, the men went to the FBI, which has been investigating the allegations. "Department officials 'don't want the violence to stop,' said Steve Rigg, the lieutenant. 'They want to [use the violence to] convince the public that we need more money, more prisons and more security'" (*San Francisco Chronicle*, October 28, October 30, November 8, November 19, and November 23, 1996).

seven

128 "Bill Irwin will [tread] the boards": From the *San Francisco Chronicle*, 1987.

132 Scoop Nisker played this tape on Kris Welch's *Morning Show* on radio station KPFA on December 3, 1987. The men made the following introductory comments:

Gabriel: "I write because it's better than staring at the blank wall. Thus far, I've found that something exists within me that isn't me, and from there I've learned that poetry brings a voice to that part of me which needs to be heard. Prison has provided me an atmosphere steeped in silence, emotion-packed moments under a scrutiny of myself, thus a voice echoes out from there . . . "

Elmo: "I mostly write about being in prison. Long-term incarceration is a unique and painful experience and there's no way anyone who hasn't lived through it can ever understand it. Yet they try. So, in my writing I try to create images which create that experience in terms of my own feelings and perceptions, but in a way which, hopefully, will succeed in giving an accurate and universal picture of what such an experience is all about."

Spoon: "I write just to write, no reason. Writing for me is like an oasis in the desert; it quenches my thirst."

James: "Writing poetry for me is a form of therapy, a way of preserving and purging my mind, so to speak. The mind, an implement of decay and self-destruction, or the key to growth and survival. It all depends on how we use it. Here in prison, where Cyclone fences, concrete walls, and steel bars shut out most forms of physical, emotional, and psychological gratification, the power and importance of the mind is evident. Here, most of what we experience that is pleasant must take place in the mind. The feel of a woman's touch, the fragrance of jasmine on a summer day, the sound of the ocean, the taste of hot pizza and cold beer, watching children play on grass in a tree-filled park—these experiences must take place within the mind because such things are not allowed in the walls of San Quentin. Some people think this process of experiencing pleasures through mental images is no more than fantasy or a symptom of psychosis. But for me, the poet as well as the prisoner, what I see and experience in my mind is another realm of reality that sustains me in the midst of the bleak reality of prison. And both are equally real."

132 Gary Trudeau, "Waiting for Mario," *Doonesbury.*

138 "I walked into the prison": Every Sunday night during the three years I worked under the grant, I baked dozens of chocolate chip cookies. I took these to Operations, the warden's office, and the porch for both staff and prisoners. Jim Carlson teased me, advising I consider adding the cost of chocolate chips to the budget of my grant proposal!

140– "A man or woman in prison doesn't stop being human": Chief Justice
141 "Thurgood Marshall of the United States Supreme Court wrote in *Procunier v. Martinez* (argued December 3, 1973; decided April 29, 1974): "When the prison gates slam behind an inmate, he does not lose his human quality; his mind does not become closed to ideas; his intellect does not cease to feed on a free and open interchange of opinions; his yearning for self-respect does not end; nor is his quest for self-realization concluded. If anything, the needs for identity and self-respect are more compelling in the dehumanizing prison environment. Whether an O. Henry authoring his short stories in a jail cell or a frightened young in-

213

mate writing his family, a prisoner needs a medium for self-expression."
(*Procunier v. Martinez, U.S. Supreme Court Reports*, 40 L Ed., 2d, page
248 [1973].)

141 "The world of corrections": Women teaching artists and artist/facilitators often talked at Arts-in-Corrections conferences about what it was
to be a woman teaching in a male prison. We spoke of man-woman sexual attraction, of course—of our own feelings and of the feelings and actions of our students. Some women spoke of how teaching in prison
taught them to stop being what Lynnelle called a "feminine wimp," forcing them to unlearn old patterns of serving men and being only kind and
never critical.

Many of our conversations centered around how to survive working
in such a violent environment. Jan Dove, teaching artist and artist/
facilitator first at California Medical Facility, Vacaville, and then at
Northern California Women's Facility, said (in an interview with the author): "You can deal with it in your mind, but your body is going to tell
you what's really going on. When I first went to CMF, I knew that I was
going to have to get a harder shell. I knew that I would never make it, I
would be one exposed nerve, and I would die in the process. However,
I was always concerned because I need my sensitivity to be an artist. So
where do you come to the point where you say, 'Okay, I've got a thick
enough shell'? Where do you start realizing that you are like those officers that you really do not admire? Who probably grew their shells,
too, for self protection."

eight

146 The quotation in the chapter title is from *Waiting for Godot* by Samuel
Beckett.

147 "'The woman who put *Island* together'": Him Mark Lai, Genny Lim,
Judy Yung, *Island: Poetry and History of Chinese Immigrants on Angel Island 1910–1940* (San Francisco: Chinese Cultural Foundation of San
Francisco, 1980); Genny Lim, *Winter Place: Poems* (San Francisco:
Kearny Street Workshop Press, 1989).

156 "Spoon and Lotta had tried": Many men at San Quentin met women
and married while still incarcerated. Some met women through personal ads, some through friends, some noticed a woman visiting someone else in the visiting room, and some, like Spoon, met women who
worked inside.

In 1968, the Inmate Family Visiting Program began in California; it
allowed most prisoners unsupervised overnight visits with members of
their immediate family in special units on prison grounds. This includ-

ed conjugal visits with a prisoner's legal spouse. On November 1, 1996, these family visits were discontinued for many prisoners (including those serving life sentences without a parole date, those guilty of narcotics trafficking while incarcerated in a state prison, those requiring close supervision, those who had committed a serious disciplinary infraction within the previous year, and those convicted of a violent offense involving a minor or family member).

nine

162 Florence Reese wrote "Which Side Are You On?" in 1931 (© 1946 [renewed] by StormKing Music, Inc.). Her husband was a rank and file organizer for the National Miner's Union in Harlan County, Kentucky.

166 "Later that year": The conversation is reproduced in Bill Moyers, *A World of Ideas* (New York: Doubleday, 1989), p. 449.

168 *Crime and Punishment in the Year 2000: What Kind of Future?* is a summary of the proceedings of the 1988 Leadership Forum sponsored by the National Council on Crime and Delinquency. NCCD is located at 685 Market St., San Francisco, California 94105; phone (415) 896-6223.

171 Fragments of Joan Swift's "Her Husband to Himself" are from *The Dark Path of Our Names* (Port Townsend, Wash.: Dragon Gate, 1985); fragments from "The Line-Up" are from *Parts of Speech* (Lewiston, Idaho: Confluence Press, 1978); "Spoon" appeared in *The Tiger Iris* (Rochester, N.Y.: BOA Editions, 1999).

178 "The War of Vaslav Nijinsky" is from Frank Bidart, *In The Western Night: Collected Poems 1965–1990* (New York: Farrar, Straus & Giroux, 1990).

ten

181 "Crack is the only thing": These words of Joseph Marshall are also included in *Street Soldier.*

182 "Chris explained how": Chris's analysis is similar to that of Geoffrey Canada in his excellent book *Fist, Stick, Knife, Gun: A Personal History of Violence in America* (Boston: Beacon Press, 1995).

Gary Webb, a staff writer for the *San Jose Mercury News*, wrote a series titled "Dark Alliance" (August 18–20, 1996). He drew from a range of sources (court and other public documents, and interviews with government officials as well as some of the criminals involved) to report that Nicaragua's Contras, with CIA complicity, raised funds for their war against Nicaragua's Sandinista regime by selling Colombian cocaine at discount rates in Los Angeles, thus helping the Crips and Bloods, the two major street gangs in the LA area, create a crack cocaine industry. And since federal sentencing guidelines punish crack cocaine users, who tend to be black, far more severely than powder users, who tend to be white, the numbers of blacks in prison is steadily rising. (In 1993 crack smokers received a three-year sentence, while coke snorters got three months [*Mercury News*, August 20, 1996].)

182 "Homeboy/Homegirl": In *Father Greg and the Homeboys*, author Celeste Fremon includes another poem, one written by an anonymous girl, to commemorate the death of an unnamed homeboy. The poem begins with the line "I am not a metaphor or a symbol." Coties knew that, as the girl's poem says, his children and other children were not "metaphors or symbols." As the girl's poem forces us to recognize, it is not a cat being "maimed in the street," but our actual children.

For other work documenting the lives of many of our young people, see Alex Kotlowitz, *There Are No Children Here: The Story of Two Boys Growing Up in the Other America* (New York: Doubleday, 1991), and Jonathan Kozol, *Amazing Grace: The Lives of Children and the Conscience of a Nation* (New York: Harper Perennial, 1993).

184 "Who survived to write his classic": Piri Thomas, *Down These Mean Streets* (New York: Alfred A. Knopf, 1967).

184 Lucille Clifton, *The Good Woman: Poems and a Memoir 1969–1980* (Brockport, N.Y.: BOA Editions, 1987).

187 "A National Town Meeting: D.C./Divided City," *Nightline*, April 27, 1989 (Show 2069, ABC News).

195 "It remains important": Daniel Berrigan, *Lights On in the House of the Dead: A Prison Diary* (Garden City, N.Y.: Doubleday, 1974).

196 "In 1992, Will received a letter": Prior to 1983, a prisoner in California could have a release date for years, and when that date arrived, he would be paroled. In 1983, the Work-Incentive Program (WIP) was implemented (a program known as day-for-day—one day *off* a prisoner's sentence for every day he or she worked).

Day-for-day sounds simple, but in fact WIP has complex formulae for credit loss and credit restoration, good-time credits versus work-time credits, etc. In practice, most prisoners serving sentences of more than three or four years who opted to participate in WIP faced constant changes in their release dates. For all prisoners whose crimes were committed after the inception of WIP, participation in this system of computing release dates is mandatory.

197 "In Borofsky and Glassman's video": James's words, spoken in *Prisoner*, were reproduced in *Artforum International*, March 1988, p. 97.

198 "'David chose five smooth stones'": Elmo's reference to David is from the Bible, 1 Sam. 17:40.

199 In *Father Greg and the Homeboys,* author Celeste Fremon writes: "In the
simplest of terms, Greg's work with the homies can be described as light-
ing a pilot light. For most of these kids, the pilot light of hope burns
very low or has gone out altogether. With love, jobs, schooling, and
sometimes a place to live, Greg relights the pilot light. Inevitably it goes
out. So he lights it again. Again it goes out. Again he lights it. And so
goes the cycle. Then one day—if everyone is lucky—the light stays on
of its own accord."

When asked why he does what he does, Father Greg is "silent for sev-
eral moments before he finally admits the obvious: 'Because I love them.
Because I love the kids.' He says it low, anguished, as if expecting pun-
ishment. Then he laughs sadly, 'But love's not very politically correct
these days . . . is it?'"